The Far Corner

The Far Corner

NORTHWESTERN VIEWS
ON LAND, LIFE, AND LITERATURE

John Daniel

COUNTERPOINT

BERKELEY

LIBRARY OF CONGRESS CATALOGING-IN-PUBLICATION DATA

Daniel, John, 1948–
    The far corner : Northwestern views on land, life, and literature /
John Daniel.
        p. cm.
    ISBN-13: 978-1-58243-493-3
    ISBN-10: 1-58243-493-X
    1. Northwest, Pacific — Description and travel. 2. Lifestyles —
Northwest, Pacific. 3. Daniel, John, 1948 — Philosophy. 4. Human ecology
— Northwest, Pacific. 5. Natural history — Northwest, Pacific. I. Title.

    F852.3.D36 2008
    979.5'044 — dc22

                                        2008048764

Cover and interior design by John Laursen at Press-22, Portland, Oregon
Printed in the United States of America

COUNTERPOINT
2117 Fourth Street
Suite D
Berkeley, CA 94710

www.counterpointpress.com

Distributed by Publishers Group West

10 9 8 7 6 5 4 3 2 1

For Jack Shoemaker,
the Lazarus of American publishing

CONTENTS

To the Reader

I have lifted my title from Stewart Holbrook, the twentieth-century Oregon wordsmith, raconteur, lowbrow historian (a phrase he either invented or happily accepted), and proponent of sustainable forestry and sensible growth before the state became broadly identified with those values. The man liked loggers, he liked trees, and he liked language, which made him a pretty complete Oregonian.

From the 1920s into the 1950s, Holbrook's books and articles sent the Pacific Northwest into the awareness and imaginings of a national readership. He tagged his beloved region the "Far Corner of America," by which he meant Oregon, Washington, and Idaho, "with a piece of western Montana thrown in for good measure." The full Northwest, to my mind, also includes southern British Columbia and northern California down at least through the Klamath Mountains and Mount Lassen, but this collection hews pretty closely to the Holbrook standard—traces of Idaho and Montana, bits of Washington, lots of Oregon.

Like Stewart Holbrook, I came to the Northwest from the far East—forty-two years ago—and called it home. It was in this region as a young man that I slowed down long enough to notice where I was and to feel somehow part of it, and it was here that I became a poet and a writer. I have made a name mainly as a nature writer, but along the way I've discovered that *Homo sapiens* is one of the most mysterious and interesting of animal species, and I know it better than I know any of the rest. I have also come to see what should have been obvious all along—that nature and human beings have been and must be inseparable. Removing ourselves from the rest of creation has gained us only a reckless disregard for other lives and a vast loneliness endured by no other species on the planet.

I have identified this book regionally because, like most authors — though many don't know it or acknowledge it — I am a regional writer. Most of what I have made in language, especially since the late 1980s, involves Northwestern places, issues, and living things. That is not to say that I intend this collection solely for a Northwestern audience. The work of an essayist is to think on the page about something that has excited his imagination, seeking to explicate, clarify, and bring it into focus — for himself, in the course of writing, and if he succeeds for himself he stands a chance to succeed for any reader of any region who's willing to make the journey. The universal can be approached only through the particular. My aim always is to write for a reader who does not know me, might live anywhere, is a good listener, and is just a tad smarter than I am.

Except for "Wavewash," which dates from the 1970s, these essays were written since publication of my first collection, *The Trail Home*, in 1992. They include meditations and arguments on old-growth forest and the practice of clearcutting; on becoming a writer; on the joys and virtues of life lived on the move; on the relationship of darkness to creativity and spirituality; on the fluid workings and biotic diversity and mythic resonance of rivers; on the writers Ken Kesey and Wallace Stegner; on the literary genre of "creative nonfiction" and its kinship with fiction; on the al-Qaeda attacks of September 11, 2001; on a stint of hot-weather solitude in the Rogue River Canyon; on death and dying and the consolations of death and dying; and on my allegiances to my home places, my state and region, and my country.

I am all too aware that the mere glimpse or mention of the word *essay* — the "e word" — is likely to spark fear in the hearts of half my readers (as it does publishers) and put the other half instantly to sleep. The reputation of the essay has been more or less ruined by dry exercises of that label assigned too often over the years in schools. Reader, if you hesitate for that reason, I hope you will forge ahead. I can't promise that you will like this work, but the contemporary personal essay is not the trussed and embalmed critter you have rightly learned to despise. Here and there it might give off a whiff of the academy, but only as part of a broader engagement with everyday life in its wholeness. The personal essay can be the most lively and welcoming of literary forms.

Whether or not my book is for you, to find an essayist who interests you is to go for a walk with a friendly (if sometimes contentious) stranger with whom you enjoy conversing on a variety of subjects, sometimes debating, sometimes agreeing, a companion whose reflections may stir you to reflect on your own experience and the questions most important to you and to your place on Earth.

John Daniel
Winter Creek, Oregon

I

Loose on the Land

CUTTINGS

Sometimes the fallers would be working on a distant slope where we could see them, and when I wasn't wrestling a choker around a log I'd watch them drop the Douglas firs. As a tree toppled and then fell faster, its boughs would sweep back, the whole trunk would flex a little just before it hit the hillside, a flash of wood showing if it broke somewhere. Across the distance the sound came late, and small. The saws sounded like hornets.

The fallers worked in pairs, and they worked slowly. It's a dangerous job — the trees are big, the hills are steep. On any one day they never seemed to advance very far against the front of forest, but they worked steadily, and day by day they got the job done. They drove the back roads every morning, they laid the big trees down, they bucked them into standard lengths. All across Weyerhaeuser's Northwest empire, they turned the standing woods into pick-up sticks.

———◆———

There are forests on the rainy side of the Cascade Range where the best way you can walk is on the trunks of fallen trees. Some of them are thicker through than you are tall. They make a random pathway through devil's club and thimbleberry, one to another and another, leading you nowhere except to more trunks with upthrust roots, more standing moss-coated stubs and skeletal snags, more bigleaf maples and western hemlocks and tall Douglas firs, and maybe a pocket of western red cedars. The bark of the big trees is pocked and charred, and most of them lean, already beginning their eventual fall. The filtered light is clear and deep. The only sound you hear is the stepping of your feet among ferns and seedling trees that grow out of the softening sapwood of their ancestors. And when you climb down from the pathway of trunks, your feet sink into a yielding matrix of moss and needles and rotting wood — trees becoming earth, earth becoming trees, the forest falling and gathering itself, rising from the abundance of its dying.

———•———

Up on the landing the steel tower stands a hundred feet tall, a diesel yarder at its base with a reel of heavy cable. When we've set the chokers and scrammed out of the way, the rigging slinger sounds his whistle. The yarder roars, the chokers cinch, and two or three logs start stubbornly up the hill like things alive, plunging and rolling, snagging on stumps and lurching free, dragging and gouging the soil, then dangling in air as they approach the landing, where they're deftly dropped in a neat deck for the waiting trucks. Everything goes to the landing — butt-cuts ten feet through, mature saw logs, buckskin snags, measly pecker-poles, even half-rotted slabs and splintered chunks. The operation scours the hillside, as far as the cables can reach, and by the time we lower the tower and trundle along to a fresh show, only stumps and sticks and boughs are left, patches of sun-struck fern and sorrel, long raw furrows in the barren ground.

———•———

Like the sea, like the streams full of salmon, the ancient forest gave plenty — totem poles, tool shafts, bows, fishing floats, baskets, dishes, robes, roots, tubers, medicine. A good red cedar might be felled by storm, or the people would bring a tree down themselves by burning into its base. They hollowed the trunk with adzes, heated water in the cavity with hot stones, stretched out the softened sides with thwarts, lashed stern and bowsprit to the hull with cedar rope. For their houses they split cedar logs into wide boards, tapping horn or hardwood wedges with a hammerstone. And sometimes they split one large plank from a standing tree and let the tree live on. The trees still live on. Here and there in the silence of the coastal forest you can find them, you can stand in an alcove where human hands selected a careful portion of what the tree could give.

———◆———

We started out from Bagby Hot Springs in Mount Hood National Forest. As I remember the trail, it climbed along a streambed and topped out on a sunny ridge, then turned north with easy ups and downs through fir and hemlock, gray cliffs on the right. We walked a day like that and camped in thicker woods where patches of old snow remained and small sounds stirred around our sleeping bags. In the morning after breakfast we walked on, following the trail toward no certain destination. We climbed for a while, still in trees, and then saw light ahead—a meadow, we thought, or a small lake. We walked into a glare of stumps and piled boughs, sap-smell heavy in the air. We worked around the far edge of the cut, trying to pick up the trail. We found the logging road, of course—dry and dusty white, unearthed boulders by its side—but we never found the trail. We sat on stumps a while and walked back the way we had come.

I was new to the Northwest then. I'd been hearing about multiple use on the public lands, and now I knew what multiple use was. I decided that even a college dropout could find better things to do than set chokers for a living.

———◆———

The rain shadow east of the Cascades is the native home of the yellow-bellies, ponderosa pines that can measure up to eight feet through and a hundred and sixty feet tall. Where they've been left alone they tilt from the earth like great orange arrows, fletched with green, parceled out in a spacious array contrived through centuries by shallow soils and periodic sweeps of mild fire.

Logging here is usually called selective, like the fires, and sometimes that's what it is. But clearcuts aren't too hard to find. The Forest Service has called them "group selections," and little blowdown patches sold for salvage have had a way of expanding into sheared squares. The pine forest stands on gentle terrain. It's easy to get at. By the 1930s many of the old yellow-belly groves were gone—*clean-cut*, in the usage of the day, the fat logs hauled out under ten-foot wheels. Now they're skidded out on chokers behind big Cats, and in most of ponderosa country, selective logging means that every thirty years or so the Cats drag out the biggest trees. It's called creaming, or high-grading, and it doesn't take everything. But the forest any kid sees is lesser than the one her father saw, diminishing toward little trees and big stumps, the ancient woods gradually brought down to human scale.

———————————•———————————

Junipers are stubby trees full of branches, and they often have several trunks. In most of them the grain is twisted, a natural tendency accentuated by the big Great Basin winds. A man had to walk many dry hills and search many canyons to find a straight-grained tree, or a tree with one straight-grained trunk inside a thicket of outer trunks. He carefully stripped a length of bark to inspect the wood. With chiselstone and hammerstone he notched the top and bottom of the stave he wanted, about four feet long, two-and-a-half inches wide. He went away then, for a few years maybe, while the stave seasoned on the tree. When he came back, if it had seasoned well, he split it from the tree with a tool of stone or antler. He carved and steamed and worked the stave until it curved in a deep belly and recurved at the ends. He boiled horn for glue, glued on sinew fibers for strength and spring. He glued on rattlesnake skin to protect the backing, fashioned a grip of wrapped buckskin. He strung the bow with a length of sinew.

One juniper, a huge tree with several great trunks and limbs, shows scars of twelve staves removed. A scar heals as the tree lays in new wood, straight-grained wood laid down where straight-grained wood was taken. One scar shows evidence of having yielded four staves in sequence. The harvest interval was probably longer than a human life. In a crotch of one of the tree's big limbs, a hammerstone remains where it was placed.

———————◆———————

Adams, St. Helens, Jefferson, Three Sisters, Diamond Peak—it doesn't matter which Cascade mountain you climb. From any summit you see a few singular volcanoes ranging away to north and south, studding an expanse of rolling green going blue in the distance. From most of the peaks you can see a lake, or several lakes. And always, on both flanks of the range and sometimes high up toward the crest, white squiggles of roads and geometric patches of sheared ground will dominate your view. From the highways you see mostly trees. From the summits you can see where all those trucks are coming from. And most of the acreage in your view is public land, retained in the ownership of the American people, part of a national forest system established over a hundred years ago to hold good woodlands in reserve against the aggressions of the timber barons.

The roads and cuts on public lands are advancing less quickly now than they did twenty years ago. Some of the cuts have greened up with genetically selected Douglas firs, fields of identical clones that will be cropped in sixty or eighty years — or sooner — and the fields planted again, to raise another forest if they can. Some of the cuts are mostly bare or brushy, flecked with silver whiskers of culled wood. From this elevation they look neat and trim. Whenever I see them I search for a metaphor. Their patchwork isn't a quilt, not yet at least, and a quilt covers, it doesn't strip. "Cascade crewcut" is a term you sometimes hear, but these cuts are worse than the ones kids show off at the malls. *Mange* is the best I've been able to do, a mange spreading through the mountains. But mange is scraggly and uneven. These clearcut patches are regular, geometric, clean-sided. Whatever's making them is working surgically. Mange doesn't know what it's doing to the dog. What's working at these mountains knows exactly what it's doing.

As my friend grows older he finds himself a farmer turning into a forester. He walks his wooded hillside, which about the time of his birth was cleared and planted in crops. The topsoil ran away, the fields were left to scrub, and now he walks among the young trees that are reclaiming the hill. He names their kinds, delighting in their company. "Look at that oak there, isn't it pretty? That'll be an oak for a long time." He tells about a neighbor who long ago swung his dog on one of the wild grape vines, a story that ends badly for the dog but brings laughter to the hillside decades later. Stories grow here like the trees.

My friend comes to walk sometimes, and other times to work. Low stumps are visible where he has thinned, the poles and logs hauled out behind his horses, seasoning now in neat piles below. In his mind he sees that cut wood forward to its good uses — fence posts, rafters, fuel for the winter — and the standing forest too grows on in his mind. "If I cut that sassafras," he says, "the little oak might grow." He opens small spaces for the sun, opens and raises his hillside forest toward the beauty of the great hardwoods that once stood here, sunlight playing in their broad leaves, their roots grown deep in the rich soil of their making.

"No, it ain't pretty," a man said to me once, "but it's the only way to harvest these trees. It don't pay to go in there just for a few." We were standing in the rainy morning outside the Weyerhaeuser time shack. His tin hat battered by years in the woods, a lunch pail and steel thermos of coffee in his hands, he spoke those words with a certainty I remember clearly — just as I remember what a good man he was, how he cussed beautifully and told fine stories and was friendly to a green chokersetter, how he worked with an impossible appetite that left me panting and cussing unbeautifully behind him. I don't remember what I or someone said that drew his response, or whether he was answering some doubt he himself had raised.

I only recall the authority of his voice, the rain dripping from his tin hat, and the idling crummies waiting to carry us out the muddy roads from camp, out through the stripped hills to another day of work.

The voice that spoke those words is my voice too. It's in all of us—the voice of practicality and common sense, the voice that understands that ugly things are sometimes necessary. It values getting a hard job done, making an honest living, and providing needed goods that all of us use. The voice has behind it certain assumptions, certain ideas about progress, economy, and standard of living, and it has behind it the evidence of certain numbers, of payrolls and balance sheets, of rotation cycles and board footage. But it is not a heartless voice. It has love for wife and children and community in it, a concern for their future. It has love for the work itself and the way of life that surrounds the work. And it has at least a tinge of regret for the forest, a sense of beauty and a sorrow at the violation of beauty.

I must have nodded, those years ago, when a good man spoke those words. I didn't argue. Against his experience and certainty, I had only a vague uneasiness. Now, I suppose, I might argue, but I know that arguing wouldn't change his mind. As he defined the issue, he saw it truly. Many of us define the issue differently now, and we think we see it truly, and all of us on every side have studies and numbers and ideas to support what we believe. All of us have evidence.

The best evidence, though, is not a number or idea. The land itself is not a number or idea, and the land has an argument to make. Turn off the highway, some rainy day in the Northwest, and drive deep into a mountain forest on the broad gravel roads and the narrow muddy roads. Drive in the rain through one of the great forests of Earth. Drive past the stands that are left, drive past the slopes of little trees and big stumps. Pass the yellow machines at rest, the gravel heaps and sections of culvert pipe, the steel drums here and there, a piece of choker rusting in a ditch. Drive until the country steepens around you, until you come to a sheer mountainside stripped of its trees—you will come to it—where puke-outs have spewed stone rubble across the road.

Stand in the rainfall, look at the stumps, and try to imagine the forest. You will have to imagine it, because on a slope this steep, with such thin soil, centuries will pass before a forest of that scale stands again, if it ever stands at all. Imagine the great Douglas firs and hemlocks spiring skyward, the bigleaf maples beneath them, and the ferns and salal of the forest floor. Imagine the creatures, great and small, weaving their countless strands of energy into a living, shifting tapestry, from deep in the rooted soil through all the reaches of shaded light to the crowning twig-tips with their green cones. The trees are gone. Many of the creatures are gone. And the very genius of these hills, that gathered the rain and changing light of untold seasons, that grew and deepened here as it brought forth a green and towering stillness, it too is leaving. It's washing down in gullies to a muddy stream.

WAVEWASH

May 22, 1978

The bridge over Dickey Creek has been closed to cars, unsafe, so it's a one-mile hike to Rialto Beach over a paved road-turned-footpath. I like the serene incongruity of traipsing the yellow center line of an autoless strip of pavement, my breathing the only engine sound, listening to liquid bird calls and the still-distant surf-boom of the sea. The asphalt is crumbling at the edges, and here on my left a slide has taken a third of its width into the Quilayute River, where a great blue heron stands in black water. To my right a jungly forest, mixed broadleafs and conifers with a lush undergrowth, presses in on the pavement. To my eyes, accustomed to the semi-arid landscape of eastern Oregon, it seems too verdant. The rainforest and river are reclaiming the road, though, which I can only count as progress.

As I tramp in with the forty-odd pounds in my backpack, three ravens lift noiselessly out of the picnic area parking lot. The automobile pull-ups, of tidy concrete, wait for business. I hike past moss-filmed picnic tables, up the high-water gravel hump at the rear of the beach, and stand squinting at mild breakers and a vast litter of bleached-silver drift logs. *Sunglasses.* Damn it. But I won't go back to the truck. It's taken me too long to get going today, what with a trip from the night's campground back to the town of Forks to buy drugstore medicine for the cold I feel coming on.

I am more moved than usual at the sight of the sea, maybe because this time I had to walk to reach it, but I resist a melodramatic gesture of greeting. We have four days to get close. I am periodically drawn to the ocean — to its edge, anyway — by a force I only vaguely understand. I need not only to see it, but to hear and smell and touch it. Maybe the body longs to return to its source; we are, after all, upright tanks three-quarters filled with seawater. We and all things alive are drops of the ocean that have busied themselves with colonizing the continents. Or maybe it's simply that the meeting of land and sea is uniquely beautiful. Borderlands are always interesting country, and seacoast is the most dramatic, dynamic, and definitive of borders.

This particular stretch of coast, the twenty miles between Rialto Beach and Cape Alava on the northern Olympic Peninsula, has been beckoning since my first visit to the Olympic in the late 1960s. Hiking the Hoh River Trail into the alpine interior to climb Mount Olympus, I noticed the separate green-shaded strip of coastal national park on my map, no roads near. Roadless coast . . . plenty in British Columbia and Alaska, not a lot here below. California has two or three patches, Oregon only some dabs, and Washington this twenty-mile stretch I intend to hike plus fifteen more to the south — the last of thirteen hundred miles of Pacific Coast that remain unviewable at scenic roadside pull-offs.

The sea is green and gentle, small breakers slapping halfheartedly, pulling back with brief choruses of chattering stones. It feels faintly silly to be walking a sun-bright beach in the burdensome traces of mountain backpacking. After experimenting with upper- and middle-beach hiking, I find it easiest to follow the firm sand footing near the wet-line, dodging the occasional ambitious sortie of foam. I head up the beach now and then to sit on a marooned snag and make notes, in case I want to write about this trip. Not that there will be much to write about. This is not an expedition to far Alaska or the Patagonian heights. I squint against the glare, nagged by the forgotten sunglasses. How have I become so dependent on so many things? Offshore a covey of little storms sprout darkly, vague mushroom clouds topping columns of rain.

I see clawed tracks in the sand, big. Bear visions rise — they come down in the evening to forage the tidepools, I have read in the Park Service pamphlet. For now, though, I am occupied with multiple sightings of a different species, brightly various in form and color—I have identified, among others, *Joy, Downy, Purex, Mr. Clean, Olympia* beer ("It's the Water"), *Bubble-Up, Snackmate* pasteurized processed cheese food, and myriad more venerable containers whose adventures in the waves have cleansed them of personal identity. Also, littered everywhere, bits and chunks and strips and gobbets of styrofoam. This beach has been taken. The invasion proceeds. Flotsam of the more traditional kind—frayed snarls of rope, splintered timbers, rust-caked pieces of metal sprouting from the sand here and there like shrubs—seems stoically native, natural to the scene. Unlike throwaway packaging, it comes of work humans do on the sea.

Ahead to the north, the little storms are converging with shore, darkening my way. I put on my parka, wolf down some gorp. Half a mile later I hear barking, the sound almost obliterated in the now-louder barrages of surf. I scan the waves for the bald heads of seals, and my eyes light on a big German shepherd berating the waves from a log a few hundred feet upcoast—the beast I wanted to make a bear, I realize, as I see more of his tracks. I trudge past, sheepish. A man and woman wave briefly from their driftwood nest at the head of the beach, then go back to sea-gazing. Herman Melville identified their type—our type—in the first chapter of *Moby-Dick*: *Posted like silent sentinels, thousands upon thousands of mortal men fixed in ocean reveries. . . .*

I look back from the first headland, Hole-in-the-Wall, which the high tide has forced me to climb instead of round. Another couple, with framepacks, is gaining on me. Intruders on my solitude. How far will I have to hike to lose my fellow humans and find my real bear? A few fat drops spatter on the stones and the rain moves south, leaving open sky, dumpling clouds. Time for cutoffs and lunch. Seaward, breakers spout against distant stacks in silent bursts, dream-surf, and beyond the stacks a ship beats north—a model, a cutout propped on the horizon. It moves with startling speed in this realm where nothing happens fast. The work underway here — the stone smoothing, the stack sculpting, the excavation and deposit of sand — has no business with human time.

The couple passes as I reduce by huge chomps an avocado and cream cheese on whole wheat sandwich, a store-bought first-day luxury. We exchange smiles, intruders all.

Later, as I round a rocky point, my eyes downcast to chart footing for my gimpy right ankle, I catalogue the varieties of styrofoam. Aptly for an American coast, it occurs predominantly in pink, white, and blue, with infrequent specimens of yellow or green. The youthful population, smooth of surface and faintly lustrous, is only beginning to give up its pre-ocean life, identifiable as bits of coffee cup, egg carton, hamburger box; beads that once filled beanbag chairs and shipping crates; hunks of ice chest and fishing float and blocks that once cushioned electronic equipment from the shocks of transit. The mature specimens are dull, weak-colored, visibly waveworn. And the ancient ones, the old growth of the genus, nameless slabs and gobs textured like large-curd cottage cheese, have shed their original incarnations and metamorphosed, like clouds, into vague creatures of imagination. How long can this stuff live? Decades, certainly. Centuries? We feed it to the ocean and she spits it back, mouthed but undigested.

Voices . . . More backpackers, rounding the point from the north. I write in my notebook: *This roadless coast is a road.* I clear the point to behold, offshore, a range of minaret stacks, up-jutting like bared foaming teeth. The tide in retreat, I ditch my pack and wander the slippery green low-tide fields, watching hermit crabs tussle in tidepools, the mild waves sliding up through little channels in the level basalt substrate.

A half-mile on, three beer-bellied men sit shirtless on a log, swilling water from a canteen. I ask if their trip is going well. *Trip?* they stare, and I notice uneasily the machetes hanging from their belts. They are surveying the national park boundary a mile inland, they tell me, and have hacked through the prodigious tangle of northland jungle for an after-work look at the sea. Melville might have made much of that, but these men would have no use for him and have only little for the Olympic coast. They grin contemptuously when I tell them that I drove four hundred miles to backpack here. Their joyless exhaustion embarrasses me. The labor I am doing is mild by comparison and completely voluntary. They are protecting my playground; their sweat and disenthusiasm safeguard my pleasure.

The Chilean Memorial Shelter, tucked into woods in a small cove, is full of campers and I do not stop. I will round Cape Johnson while the tide is low and pitch my tent on the next beach. A bald eagle, head flashing, glides north ahead of me. It occurs to me that I should at least have paused to read the marker for the drowned Chilean sailors, shipwrecked close offshore in 1920.

Around the cape in twilight I find a narrow beach fronting short, bluish clay bluffs and impenetrable forest. One sandy spot is big enough for the tent but too close to the high-water line. I may be drawn to the ocean, this mother I left long ago, but I'm also afraid of it. It seems an alien element, a darkly powerful and somehow purposeful force. I would never make a sailor. I get seasick. I am a landsman, emphatically. I tramp ahead, thinking of the Chileans, growingly anxious. It must be eight o'clock; plans for a leisurely evening of ocean watching are dashed. I curse the compulsion for solitude that has me stumbling along a darkening shore with the likely prospect of a bivouac up in the rocks or rainforest, for which I have no machete.

When I know I must stop and make some kind of camp, it appears: a cozy sand plot safely nested at the head of a beach behind a barricade of drift logs. Rain falls again as I level sand with a board; I retreat and huddle beneath the root arch of a behemoth log. No color in the sunset, but the sea is magical now, brimming quicksilver, stacks jutting in stark relief. Gulls perch quietly, absorbed in the scene. I'm still angry at my poor camp-finding, for having so little time before dark to take in what I came for. Then I realize I am taking it in, and eventually I will get the tent up, too.

Too tired for much cooking, I boil some potatoes and eat them with margarine, bean sprouts, and melted cheddar, taking sloshes from a canteen of ruby cabernet. As I sprawl on my pad in the candlelit dome, it's pleasant to imagine how it might look from the sea: a soft orange ember in the rocks and wood-wrack. Ebbing and flooding with its own tides, light-tapping rain lifts me now and then from a hard sleep. In the deep of the night the high-tide breakers pound close. I half-dream them surging phosphorescent white, eager to swirl and lift the tent away. Each wave withdraws with a shrill clatter of stones pulled seaward, chanting a truth I do not know. A pause, then — the background ocean rumble, local sloshings and streamings — and the next wave breaks. Again and again, floating, it seems, I wake and curl back into sleep.

May 23

Stuffy with the cold, still on a late-night writing rhythm — trying-to-write rhythm, I should say — I don't wake till eleven, and it's half past noon before I strap on my pack and limp north on my sore ankle, playing footsie with the high-tide foamers. The ankle, which I crunched two years ago in a rock climbing fall and surgery has helped only slightly, feels better once I've walked some of the stiffness out of it. When the rain turns from sprinkle to a heavier spatter, I climb the beach, clamber up the jumble of drift logs, and crouch under an alder thicket. The little trees are tilted seaward, as if in duel with the ceaseless waves. I sit still, facing an open gray immensity, quiet for the first time. My mind is clear of AM radio tatters. No compulsion to move ahead, no desire to eat or plan or write, and no cheap vanities or self-indictments, those sand fleas that pester my head. For the moment I am a stone, a log. The ocean rounds my edges.

Climbing the steep points the tide won't allow me to turn, I thrash through wet vegetation, grabbing stems and tufts to pull myself up, getting raked now and then by spiny devil's club, inhaling thick plant-breath raised by the re-emerged sun. The beaches between points are hard-packed sand pavement. No other hikers today, and even the styrofoam hordes have thinned. My coast at last. I salute a squadron of gulls, shout howdy to a lone seal. The waves, in no hurry, erase my tracks behind me.

Rounding a brief unclimbable point as the tide comes in, I am forced to rock-hop, tuning in to the rhythm of waves to gauge which dry perch I can gain before the next one charges. The game has some urgency—if I don't get around the point before the tide floods full, I might not get around it at all—but it's a small one compared to the hardest of the vertical climbing dramas I used to contrive, in which every move was its own crisis. This game is sweeter in simple pleasure.

Fifty feet up on a forested shelf, a square corner in the undergrowth catches my eye. I shed my pack and scramble up the bank, hoping— suddenly a child—to find the shelter and bleached bones of a Chilean sailor. No remains, but what a campsite—neat rock fire-ring, a windscreen of drift boards, a clearing just big enough for the tent, and a framed-in-spruces picture window of an exquisite collection of surf-spouting stacks. A short walk to the north a stream flows, where gulls throng to pluck worms or other dainties tumbling seaward in the tannic water.

While still debating the part of me that wants to stick to the plan, *hike a few more miles*, I know this is my place. The plan was to pack the twenty miles to Cape Alava in three days and hitchhike back to the truck on the fourth, but my ankle is hurting, and on the Olympic's back roads it might be more hiking than hitching. Most of all, though, I realize that I crave a quiet visit with the sea, no pack frame squeezing my vertebrae and laboring my breath and bumping the back of my head when I try to watch a bird in flight. I will camp here, day-hike farther north tomorrow, and the next day—or when my food runs out—I'll pack out the way I came.

The achiever in me continues to protest—*defeat, cop-out*—but I know I can outlast him. Every once in a while I need to hike not in a group, not with friend or lover, but in my own society. And society it is—alone, wherever I go I keep bumping into myself. In two days I will turn thirty, a prospect I'm not entirely at peace with. Earlier this month I quit a comfortable railroad job I'd held for seven years. I've been trying to write, off and on, for three years. Next to nothing published. One story, in a climbing magazine, for sixty dollars—I photocopied the check—and a ragged piece of work at that. Nothing much accomplished of any kind, really, in my thirty years, less two days, on the planet. The achiever won't be silenced about that, and is he wrong?

At home I tossed into my pack an envelope of psilocybin mushrooms that had lain in a dresser drawer for three years. I haven't taken a psychedelic for a long time. What the hell, I decide, and chew the mushrooms down with gorp and water. Doubting their potency, I pitch the tent and set up camp, then lie in the sun on my sleeping pad. The mushrooms have altered my mind only with a miserable headache, or maybe that's just the cold. A walk seems the only remedy, and as I descend to the beach I notice how vast and bright and airy the windy space around me seems, how the crying and veering seagulls are such . . . *seagulls*, and soon I am crouched and gazing at a tidepool of anemones that won't quite hold still—like flowers they seem, vaginas, medusa heads, radiant starbursts.

I head for the sea, traversing the flank of a tree-plumed stack that has become a low-tide isthmus, wildly amused at the notion that *Old mushrooms never die, and I am fading away* . . . I thank the barnacles for giving grip to my boots, then laugh that I just spoke aloud to barnacles. For a while the scrambling gets hard. I shiver in a shadowed cleft, unsure how to continue, thinking I might have to go back. Without thought, though, my hands and feet climb me up a short steep face and suddenly, with a smack of wind and sun on my face, the open spangled sea lies before me, alive with slow combing swells that seem to move within me as they move without, rising and dipping away, foaming on a rock shelf below, pouring back, gathering to surge again.

I sit, laved in sunny breeze. This is the way things are, so brilliantly fluidly full of themselves, and I always forget, I always fall from this knowing. How could I or anyone not worship this cauldron of shining energy, this ceaseless pluming power, this ocean that bore us? There is nothing I need. I breathe as easily as the ocean swells. After a while I hear my own voice sounding a long, low tone that mingles—perfectly, it seems—with the infinitely inflected voice of the sea.

Sometime later, as I continue my way around the stack, I squat to gaze at a pool of orange and purple starfish and giant anemones. I notice a tiny scrap of styrofoam by my boot—old, worn, almost the color of seaweed. I put it in my pocket and continue to admire the starfish, but I know I'm starting to come down. There always comes that point where the psychedelic pathway branches into duality again. Natural, unnatural. Past, future. Expanded consciousness, plain old me. The path divides and turns back on itself, forks and turns until I'm lost again in my labyrinth of familiar fears and desires and hopes and regrets, all my discordant human carings.

I dwell on the not-so-perfect elements of my world. A relationship two years ended that won't quite die within me, hanging on like a stubborn cold. The friction of my loneliness against my need to be alone. The advent of my fourth decade with few roots laid down, little direction to my drifting. I quit the cushy railroad job—criminally easy, my nearest supervisor four hundred miles away—to challenge myself, but my résumé is pretty puny when it comes to meeting challenges. I've dropped out of college, lost through my own unresponsiveness a girl I lived with for five years, taken up and abandoned the classical guitar, and fallen out of a mediocre climbing career. I want to write, but who says I *can* write?

The ocean has changed, a nervous gray energy shuttling itself to the same conclusion, slopping against stone and sliding back spent. I continue my scramble around the stack but balk at an easy but slightly crumbly stretch of wall, freaked by the rocks and gurgling water fifteen feet below. I go back the way I came, sadly convinced that five years ago I would have gone for it, but at the spot where I sat and sang to the sea—how long ago?—I stop and feel my mouth turn up in a slight smile. The sea hasn't changed. The sea is the sea, not what I project on it. It will continue to be itself, and so will I, and so will the self who sang to the sea. Forgetting that self is a game I play, maybe everyone plays, old men on the golf course, students in classrooms, me on the Olympic coast. Maybe the entire universe plays it, a somehow necessary hide-and-seek, cosmic and comic at the same time. There's only an *s* of difference.

But why the game? Why my doubts and divisions, and why can I transcend them only when I go aloft with a psychedelic drug? Everything is changed but really nothing is changed, the standard landing at the end of a trip. In the twilight I return to the beach and tread circles for a while on the scalloped, glistening sand, trying to feel like a child. As I head for camp I catch a motion in the forest front some two hundred feet to the north, a silent opening and closing, a movement immediately stilled in the dusky light.

May 24

After two days the sea and I are close enough for naked touch—a shivering splash, a long drying on a warm, silvered log. Packless, I am en route to the Norwegian Memorial, five miles north of my campsite, on a receding afternoon tide. Heavy clumps of cloud stream landward—an advance guard, I speculate. I've seen more sun in two days than a visitor here has a right to expect in a week. They don't call it rainforest for nothing.

I find no marker, only a tired stream, a mossy outhouse, and a smoky little shelter with plank bunk beds, a haven for spiders and mice. The open spruce forest abounds with signs of Boy Scout–style encampments—giant fire rings, saplings chopped off three feet above ground, scraps of foil and toilet paper. Memorials less than stirring. I eat an orange and start back, smug about my own inviolate campsite.

Sapped by the cold that's at last hitting its stride in my system, I stop for a nap, head propped on a log. My thoughts seem to drift with the blended rumble of the sea, its countless streamings and spewings. . . . Gull cry, press of sunwarmth on my face. I open my eyes to a thin fabric of cloud. I am absorbed in sand, an enormous weight with vision. *The staring unsleeping eye of the earth*, Robinson Jeffers called the Pacific. *And what it watches is not our wars.* An osprey wings overhead and hits the shallows with a careless splash; he comes up empty, pumping himself almost upright against the wind to shed the brine. In a few minutes he dives again, and this time he rises with a lively silver prize in his talons and flies for the forest behind me.

Oh, the serene brutalities of nature. A joy to watch, when it isn't oneself in the talons. I wonder about the sailors—Norwegian, Chilean, all of them. This coast is an equal-opportunity killer. Did any make it to shore? Unlikely, given those spouting stacks and not-quite-submerged reefs. Drowning must be a hideous death, if one is conscious at the point when cold drags the body down and the lungs begin to suck in water. It gives me a peculiar horror, perhaps because when I was three or four I fell into the Catawba River, in North Carolina, and flailed around underwater until my brother reached me and hauled me out.

The sea's vastness unsettles me, its formlessness and power, the way it seems to want to dissolve and swallow all it touches. And what doesn't it touch? It takes to the sky to fall on land as rain and snow, and grain by grain it carries the continents back to itself. But it's the depth that troubles me most. Both earth and air are obviously much deeper, but who imagines them so? Ocean, not land or atmosphere, is the abyss, the immeasurable depth, the primordial chaos—a bottomless region of evil spirits in mythology, little visited and far from completely charted by scientists to this day. The lowest reaches of the Pacific are total darkness and the crushing weight of three to five vertical miles of water—the largest, most remote wilderness on Earth, and not one I care to visit. I like the view from here, the borderland, the lively, glinting, changeable windswept surface.

Back at camp, at dusk, as I get supper together and drink the last of the wine, the sea is alive with lights: ships sliding along the horizon, and a swarm of sailboats, little lit triangles, closer in. The lights are lovely, but the ships disturb me. For three days I have watched their steady traffic beating north and south. Some appear to be tankers in the Alaska oil trade. Styrofoam and bleach bottles are one thing—regrettable, a blight, but a small aesthetic concern. There will always be flotsam. But this coast that claimed the Chilean and Norwegian ships, and no doubt others, will claim more in its time. It is stern, like the longer and wilder shorelines of British Columbia and Alaska, and just as defenseless against black memorials to human convenience.

My convenience. I burned oil to get here and will burn more to get home. All my backcountry trips, seeking solace in the sanity of nature, involve the consumption of oil. And what shall I do about this? I'll do what most of us will do. Nothing, as long as we can pay the price at the pump.

We will call that tanker wreck an accident when it occurs, but we could as accurately call it inevitable. What's the difference? Two years ago, a little aluminum chock I had lodged in a crack ripped loose and I fell thirty feet, pulling out other chocks, and hit a ledge full-weight with my right foot just before the rope stopped me. An accident, or a predictable result of fatigue and carelessness and limited skills? Seven years ago, a girl I'd barely known in college happened to visit the house in Berkeley where I was visiting, and we fell in love and lived together for five years. Accident? Meant to be, the romantic in me says. Three years ago, she started law school and fell in love with a professor, while I was too dense, or didn't care enough, to get it that something was wrong. Accident, or bound to happen? Twelve years ago, I arrived at college, first in my class in high school, valedictorian, Presidential Scholar, football team, and two years later I was a dropout, a draft resister, a hippie doing drugs, a West Coast drifter with not a lot of plans. . . .

I'm not sure that I've ever made a real decision in my life. Things have happened, a kind of tide, and I've gone with it, bouncing easily off any rocks—till recently—with just a bruise or two. One spring night in college, I lay for hours with a friend on the warm asphalt of Interstate 84 in the Columbia Gorge. We were hitchhiking back to Portland from an errand involving a motor scooter my friend wanted to buy. The freeway was deserted, silent, for ten or twenty minutes at a time. We had time to talk, watching the stars, and we debated my theory that the things that happen to us are good things. I acknowledged that I spoke only for my white, middle-class, college-student self. It wasn't a theory of all beings. But for me, I argued, even the painful things that had happened—chronically wetting the bed as a child, running from fights with other kids, my father's embarrassing drunkenness, his fights with my mother—were all to the good, because somehow they had brought me to where I was, eighteen years old and happy, lying with a friend beneath the stars on I-84 in the Columbia Gorge, on a warm spring night in 1967.

The years since have cast some doubt on my theory, but now, scraping the aluminum camp pot with my spoon for the last shreds of noodles and tuna with whatever, I'm of a mind to resurrect it. My father died two years ago, about the time my girlfriend left. But even then, in my anguish over both I felt streaks of a strange joy, a whiff of new beginnings, of setting out by myself on a fresh morning trail. I was off work that summer and fall with my broken ankle. Fate was cruel, I brooded melodramatically, to bunch its blows so, yet during those months I hit the bars a little less and sat at the living room table a little more, scrawling sentences in pencil and poking the keys of the Royal manual typewriter I'd bought. I jotted thoughts and descriptions in a small black loose-leaf notebook, the one I'm writing in tonight on the Washington coast. I took a turn, I hope, toward being a writer.

Spotting this campsite was another accident, so-called. A happy one. My achiever no longer is clamoring that I should have trekked on to Cape Alava, where I'd have arrived tonight or tomorrow. If my twenties have taught me anything, it may be a glimmer of understanding that the quality of my time is more important than how much I cram into it. To hurry is one response to the awareness of mortality. To slow down, to allow each moment to fill as a stream fills a pool, is starting to feel like a better way. Those injuries two years ago somehow deepened me into my life. I wish I hadn't hurt my ankle. After a day's hiking, the pain hobbles me. I never expected to walk into my thirties with a permanent limp. But it does keep me aware of every footstep.

Venus is a drop of liquid light. On the beach below, a raccoon lumbers to the water and wades the gentle shallows, pausing, nosing around, a specter melting into a patch of rocks. Beyond, breakers sweep shoreward out of the open night, swelling smoothly across a path of pale moonlight, flashing glinting silver bellies before curling overtop to collapse in luminous roils.

May 25

In my dream I ask the sea, a dark-haired woman, for a child. She gives me a smooth stone, eccentrically shaped, gray with a streak of white running through it. The stone glows as if from within. I wake with a sense of having received a treasure, and with a clogged nose and headache. Rain drums in tatters against the tent. " 'Appy birdday, John," I say aloud. I break camp without eating, load my pack, and set out southward, striding hard to beat the rising tide to Cape Johnson. (I slept till eleven again—a real nature boy.) I hike head down in overpants and hooded slicker, watching my bulky reflection on the glistening, hard-packed sand.

Sweating like a carrot in a steamer I turn the cape, a little worried but with time to spare. The rain eases and bears down again. Above me, atop a rocky bluff, the dripping forest is in its element. The seaward view is a seethe of smoky gray and black. At the Chilean Memorial cove—deserted this time—I stop at the shelter. The tide must turn before I can round the next headland. I dig out my stove and heat water for tea, flicking away impudent chipmunks as I peruse a week-old *Seattle Post-Intelligencer*. If this is post-intelligence, I query the chipmunks, what is pre-intelligence? I'm impatient. My clothes turn clammy cold.

There's a tired sameness to all trail shelters . . . spiderwebs, dingy bunks, a musty smell. A five-inch yellow slug oozes over a wet charred log in the fire ring outside, its ears—if that's what they are—waggling in slow motion. I examine its progress, which is slightly more compelling than watching the trees grow. It leaves a faint trail of slime. After a while I hear myself say, "Hey, you're my bear." It lacks charisma, this slug, it's nothing to tell stories about back home, but it's as wild and mysterious as any creature on Earth. I know nothing of how it moves, what it eats, how it makes love, how far it travels, how long it lives. I do know this: unlike me, the slug need not make special trips to the wilderness. A slow-motion life, doing exactly what it does, no dithering or regrets. A speck of consciousness, maybe, but no memory. No past, no future, no concern about aging or death.

My annoyance at having to stop here passes into a subtle pleasure. I am pinned for a while by the storm-brewing sea, a traveler taking refuge, waiting his time. To warm myself, I walk to the Chilean Memorial marker. In 1920 the *W. J. Pirrie* broke in half on offshore rocks in eighty-five-mile-an-hour winds, the entire crew swept overboard along with the captain, his wife, and their young child. Two sailors somehow made it to shore, the only survivors. Of the others, eighteen bodies washed up and were buried here in a common grave.

Today I am thirty. A lot of the drowned sailors probably weren't.

At five-thirty I push on. The tide has been ebbing for an hour, and waiting out rain in this country is like waiting for a slug to dance. Partway around the headland I stop to watch two seals bob up now and then. They look my way, as if curious. The seaweed fields, resplendent in sun three days ago, are even more beautiful in rain—a radiant lettuce-green, patched with purple-black mussel beds. Gray swells slosh languidly, a rich foaming broth. The pressure in my head has eased a little. Sooner or later in every outing—mountains, desert, anywhere—I come to the same questions. How can it be that the world is, and is exactly as it is? And how can it be that an awareness I call "I" is here to see it and wonder at it? It all seems so . . . unlikely. And so beautiful, so vastly, achingly beautiful. Earth is too perfect, too filled with glory to have been an accident, but what god, what God of gods, could have designed exactly *this*, and us as part of it, and woven suffering and death into the very fabric of splendor?

The seals pop up again, so at home they seem subtle extensions of the sea itself. And they are. *And I am too*, I remember. I crawled from the same sea they swim, and my consciousness, like theirs, is a bubble on the depths. I carry within me my own abyss, my own uncharted deep that I don't know, but it knows me. It *is* me. It's not that I've never made a decision—by the time I know what I want to do, the decision seems already formed. Thought is mostly afterthought, post-intelligence, a beam of consciousness discovering *faits accomplis* of the unconscious mind. My dark abyss is always taking in experience, more than my daylight mind can know, and guides me from within. It led me here, to this coast. It gave me the dark-haired woman, the luminous stone, the moment of singing to the sea. It gave me the sentences in my notebook, the stories and poems I've been laboring over at home. Sometimes, when I've managed to write a phrase or image that seems just right, I'll stare at it on the page and ask, where did that come from? A moment ago I didn't know what to write, then my pencil wrote. Something is alive within me, a force insistent as the tide, and it knows more than I do.

Despite my running nose and aching head I feel complete, merged with the moment, as I round the headland. Ishmael, I remember from *Moby-Dick*, didn't go to sea as a random act—he was drawn to it, repeatedly, by his own inarticulate brooding, by hungers he scarcely understood. He followed a visionary procession of whales, one of them rising like a snow hill in the air. And what did he hope to find? What did he seek? What all of us seek. The self, as Narcissus did, but more than that. The self beyond the self. *The image of the ungraspable phantom of life*, says Melville, *and this is the key to it all....*

As I make the beach south of the headland, I'm considering the possibility that as I've drifted these past few years I've been progressing, in my way, as slowly as the slug on the charred log, but maybe as surely, too. A few weeks ago I went to a psychic in Portland. She knew that I had been trying to write, which gave her instant credibility, and told me I had been trying for longer than I knew. I was a writer in previous lives, she said, never successful because I've never believed in myself. So how can I believe in myself? I asked. "Oh, that's up to you," she said with a smile. "I'm just a psychic."

I stop to sit on a log and scratch some notes, then set off at a quick pace on the hard-packed sand. As I hike the last couple of miles, I realize I have said goodbye. My interest has turned from the sea, and examining my life, to dry socks and a restaurant meal.

After disappointing fried chicken and a few birthday beers in the town of Forks, I drive south a few miles and pull east off 101 onto a logging road to spend the night. In the enclosed truck bed, I write for a while by flashlight. Then, drowsy from the cold medicine but unable to sleep, I shift and turn irritably in my sleeping bag. I usually feel settled, happy, at the end of a tramp. After a long restless time, I suddenly get it. My ears are empty. All I hear is an occasional car passing on the highway. And so from memory I recall it—the steady, ongoing rumble and pour, the deep percussion of pounding surf, the hiss and slide of the shallow foamers— the old lonesome stir of sea meeting land, and soon I feel it swirling me, slowly, into sleep.

A Word in Favor of Rootlessness

I am one of the converted when it comes to the cultural and economic necessity of finding place. Our rootlessness—our refusal to accept the discipline of living as responsive and responsible members of neighborhoods, communities, landscapes, and ecosystems—is perhaps our most serious and widespread disease. The history of our country, and especially of the American West, is in great part a record of damage done by generations of boomers, both individual and corporate, who have wrested from the land all that a place could give and continually moved on to take from another place. Boomers such as Wallace Stegner's father, who, as we see him in *The Big Rock Candy Mountain*, "wanted to make a killing and end up on Easy Street." Like many Americans, he was obsessed by the fruit of Tantalus: "Why remain in one dull plot of Earth when Heaven was reachable, was touchable, was just over there?"

We don't stand much chance of restoring and sustaining the health of our land, or of perpetuating ourselves as a culture, unless we can outgrow our boomer adolescence and mature into stickers, or nesters—human beings willing to take on the obligations of living in communities rooted in place, conserving nature as we conserve ourselves. And maybe, slowly, we are headed in that direction. The powers and virtues of place are celebrated in a growing body of literature and discussed in conferences and classrooms across the country. Bioregionalism, small-scale organic farming, urban food co-ops, and other manifestations of the spirit of place seem to be burgeoning, or at least coming along.

That is all to the good. But as we settle into our home places and local communities and bioregional niches, as we become the responsible economic and ecologic citizens we ought to be, I worry a little. I worry, for one thing, that we will settle in place so pervasively that no unsettled places will remain. But I worry about us settlers, too. I feel at least a tinge of concern that we might allow our shared beliefs and practices to harden into orthodoxy, and that the bathwater of irresponsibility we are perhaps ready to toss out the home door might contain a lively baby or two. These fears may turn out to be groundless, like most of my insomniac brood-ings. But they are on my mind, so indulge me, if you will, as I address some of the less salutary aspects of living in place and some of the joys and perhaps necessary virtues of rootlessness.

No power of place is more influential than climate, and I feel com-pelled at the outset to report that we who live in the wet regions of the Northwest suffer immensely from our climate. Melville's Ishmael experi-enced a damp, drizzly November in his soul, but only now and then. For us it is eternally so, or it feels like eternity. From October well into June we slouch in our mossy-roofed houses listening to the incessant patter of rain, dark thoughts slowly forming in the cloud chambers of our minds. It's been days, weeks, *years*, it seems, since a neighbor knocked or a let-ter arrived from friend or agent or editor. Those who live where sun and breezes play, engaged in their smiling businesses, have long forgotten us, if they ever cared for us at all. Rain drips from the eaves like poison into our souls. We sit. We sleep. We wait for the mail.

What but climate could it be that so rots the fiber of the Northwest-ern psyche? Or if not climate itself, then an epiphenomenon of climate— perhaps the spores of an undiscovered fungus floating out of those deca-dent forests we environmentalists are so bent on saving. Oh, we try to improve ourselves. We join support groups and twelve-step programs, we drink gallons of cappuccino and caffè latte, we bathe our pallid bod-ies in the radiance of full-spectrum light machines. These measures keep us from dissolving outright into the sodden air, and when spring arrives we bestir ourselves outdoors, blinking against the occasional cruel sun and the lurid displays of rhododendrons. By summer we have cured sufficiently to sally forth to the mountains and coast, where we linger in sunglasses and try to pass for normal.

But it is place we are talking about, the powers of place. As I write this, my thoughts are perhaps unduly influenced by the fact that my right ear has swollen to the size and complexion of a rutabaga. I was working behind the house this afternoon, cutting up Douglas fir slash with the chainsaw, when I evidently stepped too close to a yellow jacket nest. I injured none of their tribe, to my knowledge, but one of them sorely injured me. Those good and industrious citizens take place pretty seriously. Having no poison on hand with which to obliterate them, I started to get out the .22 and shoot them each and every one, but thought better of it and drank a tumbler of bourbon instead.

And now, a bit later, a spectacle outside my window only confirms my bitter state of mind. The place in question is the hummingbird feeder, and the chief influence of that place is to inspire in hummingbirds a fiercely intense desire to impale one another on their needlelike beaks. Surely they expend more energy blustering in their buzzy way than they can possibly derive from the feeder. This behavior is not simply a consequence of feeding Kool-Aid to already over-amped birds — they try to kill each other over natural flower patches too. Nor can it be explained as the typical mindlessly violent behavior of the male sex in general. Both sexes are represented in the fray. It is merely a demonstration of over-identification with place. Humans do it too. Look at Yosemite Valley on the Fourth of July. Look at any empty parking space in San Francisco. Look at Jerusalem.

When human beings settle in a place for the long run, much good occurs. There are dangers, though. Stickers run the substantial risk of becoming sticks-in-the-mud, and sticks with attitude. Consider my own state of Oregon, which was settled by farmers from the Midwest and upper South who had one epic move in them, across the Oregon Trail, and having found paradise resolved not to stir again until the millennium. The more scintillating sorts — murderers, prostitutes, lawyers, writers, other riffraff—tended toward Seattle or San Francisco. And so it happens that we Oregonians harbor behind our bland and agreeable demeanor a serious streak of moralism and conformism. We have some pretty strict notions about the way people should live. We were among the first to start the nationwide spate of legal attacks on gay and lesbian rights, and we annually rank among the top five states in citizen challenges to morally subversive library books, such as *Huckleberry Finn*, *The Catcher in the Rye*, and *The Color Purple*.

This pernicious characteristic is strongest, along with some of our best characteristics, where communities are strongest and people live closest to the land—in the small towns. When my girlfriend and I lived in Klamath Falls in the early 1970s, we were frequently accosted by our elderly neighbor across the road, Mrs. Grandquist. She was pointedly eager to lend us a lawn mower, and when she offered it she had the unnerving habit of staring at my hair. Our phone was just inside the front door, and sometimes as we arrived home it rang before we were entirely *through* the door. "You left your lights on," Mrs. Grandquist would say. Or, "You really ought to shut your windows when you go out. We've got burglars, you know." Not in that block of Denver Avenue, we didn't. Mrs. Grandquist and other watchful citizens with time on their hands may have kept insurance rates down, but the pressure of all those eyes and inquiring minds was at times intensely uncomfortable. Small towns are hard places to be different. Those yellow jackets are vigilant, and they can sting.

Customs of land use can become as ossified and difficult to budge as social customs. The Amish, among other rural peoples, practice responsible and sustainable farming. But long-term association with a place no more guarantees good stewardship than a long-term marriage guarantees a loving and responsible relationship. As Aldo Leopold noted with pain, there are farmers who habitually abuse their land and cannot easily be induced to do otherwise. Thoreau saw the same thing in Concord—landspeople who, though they must have known their places very well, mistreated them continually. They whipped the dog every day because the dog was no good, and that's the way no-good dogs had always been dealt with.

As for us of the green persuasions, settled or on the loose, we too are prone — more prone than most — to orthodoxy and intolerance. We tend to be overstocked in piety and self-righteousness, deficient in a sense of humor about our values and our causes. Here in the Northwest, where debate in the last twenty years has focused on logging issues, it's instructive to compare bumper stickers. Ours say, sanctimoniously, STUMPS DON'T LIE or LOVE YOUR MOTHER. Those who disagree with us, on the other hand, sport sentiments such as HUG A LOGGER — YOU'LL NEVER GO BACK TO TREES, or EARTH FIRST! (WE'LL LOG THE OTHER PLANETS LATER).

I don't mean to minimize the clear truth that ecological blindness and misconduct are epidemic in our land. I do mean to suggest that rigid ecological correctness may not be the most helpful treatment. All of us, in any place or community or movement, tend to become insiders; we all need the outsider, the contrarian, to shake our perspective and keep us honest. Prominent among Edward Abbey's many tonic qualities was his way of puncturing environmental pieties (along with almost every other brand of piety he encountered). What's more, the outsider can sometimes see a landscape with a clarity unavailable to the native or the longtime resident. It was as a relative newcomer to the Southwest that Abbey took the notes that would become his best book, in which he imagined the canyon country of the Colorado Plateau more deeply than anyone had imagined it before or has imagined it since. His spirit was stirred and his vision sharpened by his outsider's passion. I don't know that he could have written *Desert Solitaire* if he had been raised in Moab or Mexican Hat.

Unlike Thoreau, who was born to his place, or Wendell Berry, who returned to the place he was born to, Edward Abbey came to his place from afar and took hold. More of a lifelong wanderer was John Muir, whom we chiefly identify with the Sierra Nevada but who explored and sojourned in and wrote of a multitude of places, from the Gulf of Mexico to the Gulf of Alaska. I think Muir needed continually to see new landscapes and life forms in order to keep his ardent mind ignited. Motion for him was not a pathology but a devotion, an essential joy, an ongoing discovery of place and self. Marriage to place is something we need to realize in our culture, but not all of us are the marrying kind. The least happy period of Muir's life was his tenure as a settled fruit farmer in Martinez, California. He was more given to the exhilarated attention and fervent exploration of *wooing*, more given to rapture than to extended fidelity. "Rapture" is related etymologically to "rape," but unlike the boomer, who rapes a place, the authentic wooer allows the place to enrapture him.

Wooing often leads to marriage, of course, but not always. Is a life of wooing place after place less responsible than a life of settled wedlock? It may be less sustainable, but the degree of its responsibility depends on the authenticity of the wooing. John Muir subjected himself utterly to the places he sought out. He walked from Wisconsin to the Gulf Coast, climbed a tree in a Sierra windstorm, survived a subzero night on the summit of Mount Shasta by scalding himself in a sulfurous volcanic vent. There was nothing macho about it—he loved where he happened to be and refused to miss one lick of it. In his wandering, day to day and minute to minute, he was more placed than most of us ever will be, in a lifetime at home or a life on the move. As followers of the Grateful Dead like to remind us, quoting J. R. R. Tolkien, "Not all who wander are lost."

Muir's devoted adventuring, of course, was something very different from the random restlessness of many in our culture today. Recently I sat through a dinner party during which the guests, most of them thirty-something, compared notes all evening about their travels through Asia. They were experts on border crossings, train transport, currency exchange, and even local art objects, but nothing I heard that evening indicated an influence of land or native peoples on the traveler's soul. They were travel technicians. Many backpackers are the same, passing through wilderness places encapsulated in maps and objectives and high-tech gear. There *is* a pathology there, a serious one. It infects all of us to one degree or another. We have not yet arrived where we believe—and our color photographs show—we have already been.

But if shifting around disconnected from land and community is our national disease, I would argue — perversely perhaps, or perhaps just homeopathically — that it is also an element of our national health. Hank Williams and others in our folk and country traditions stir something in many of us when they sing the delights of the open road, of rambling on the loose by foot or thumb or boxcar through the American countryside. Williams's "Ramblin' Man" believes that God intended him for a life of discovery beyond the horizons. Is this mere immaturity? Irresponsibility? An inability to relate to people or place? Maybe. But maybe also renewal, vitality, a growing of the soul. It makes me very happy to drive the highways and back roads of the American West, exchanging talk with people who live where I don't, pulling off somewhere to sleep in the truck and wake to a place I've never seen. I can't defend the cost of such travel in fossil fuel consumption and air befoulment — Williams's rambler at least took the fuel-efficient train — but I do know that it satisfies me as a man and a writer.

Such pleasure in movement — the joy of hitting the trail on a brisk morning, of watching from a train the towns and fields pass by, of riding a skateboard or hang glider or even a 747 — must come from a deep and ancient source. All of us are descended from peoples whose way was to roam with the seasons, following game herds and the succession of edible plants, responding to weather and natural calamities and the shifting field of relations with their own kind. And those peoples came, far deeper in the past, from creatures not yet human who crawled and leapt and swung through the canopies of trees for millions of years, evolving prehensile hands and color binocular vision as a consequence, then took to the ground and learned to walk upright and wandered out of Africa (or so it now seems) and across the continents of Earth. Along the way, lately, we have lost much of the sensory acuity our evolutionary saga evoked in us, our ability to smell danger or read a landscape or notice nuances of weather, but the old knowing still stirs an alertness, an air of anticipation, when we set out on our various journeys.

The value of the traveler's knowing figures considerably in native cultural traditions. In Native American stories of the Northwest collected by Jarold Ramsey in *Coyote Was Going There*, I notice that Coyote doesn't seem to have a home — or if he does, he's never there. "Coyote was traveling upriver," the stories begin. "Coyote came over Neahkanie Mountain. . . ." These stories take place in the early time when the order of the world was still in flux. Coyote, the placeless one, helps people and animals find their proper places. You wouldn't want to base a code of conduct on his character, which is unreliable and frequently ignoble, but he is the agent who introduces human beings to their roles and responsibilities in life. Coyote is the necessary inseminator. (Sometimes literally.) He is the shifty and shiftless traveler who fertilizes the locally rooted bloomings of the world.

Maybe Coyote moves among us as the stranger, often odd or disagreeable, sometimes dangerous, who brings reports from far places. Maybe that stranger is one of the carriers of our wildness, one of the mutant genes that keep our evolution fresh and thriving. It is for that stranger, says Elie Wiesel, that an extra place is set at the Seder table. The voyager might arrive, the one who finds his home in the homes of others. He might tell a story, a story no one in the family or local community is capable of telling, and the children who hear that story might imagine their lives in a new way.

It could be Hank Williams who stops in, and he'll sing to you half the night, and maybe yours will be the family he needs, and he won't die of whiskey and barbiturates in the backseat of a car. Or Huck Finn might be your stranger, on the run from "sivilization," dressed as a girl and telling stupendous lies. It could be Jack Kerouac and Neal Cassady, on the road with their Beat buddies, hopped-up on speed, and they never *will* stop talking. It might be Gerry Nanapush, the Chippewa power man Louise Erdrich has given us, escaped from jail still again to slip through the mists and snows with his ancient powers. Or it might be Billy Parham or John Grady Cole, Cormac McCarthy's boy drifters. They'll want water for their horses, they'll be ready to eat, and if you're wise you'll feed them. They won't talk much themselves, but you just might find yourself telling *them* the crucial story of your life.

Or yours could be the house where Odysseus calls, a still youngish man returning from war, passionate for his family and the flocks and vineyards of home. Just as likely, though, he could be an old man when he stands in your door. No one's quite sure what became of Odysseus. Homer tells us that he made it to Ithaca and set things in order, but the story leaves off there. Some say he resumed his settled life, living out his days as a placed and prosperous landsman. But others say that after all his adventures he couldn't live his old life again. Alfred, Lord Tennyson, writes that Odysseus shipped out from Ithaca with his trusted crew. Maybe so, but maybe it wasn't just him. Maybe Penelope, island bound all those years, was stir-crazy herself. Maybe they left Telemachus the ranch and set out together across the sea, two gray spirits "yearning in desire / To follow knowledge like a sinking star, / Beyond the utmost bound of human thought."

In Praise of Darkness

A few years ago I conducted an experiment in solitude, several months apart from human news or company in a cabin in Oregon's Rogue River wilderness, and I thought I might become a morning writer. I had no electricity, no radio, no music. I left the radiotelephone switched off. Alone in the rhythms of natural light and dark, I thought I'd get up with the birds, as the writers I most admire have done, and have my workday finished by noon, the afternoon and evening mine to nibble like a well-earned apple.

It didn't happen. For four and a half months, mid-November through March, I grumbled out of bed most mornings no earlier than ten, grinding my coffee on the cabin deck while looking down, often, at two or three black-tailed deer, who looked up at me with what seemed reproach in their large liquid eyes. I read during the day and did some journal writing, walked, fished or hunted, and performed the regular chores of garden, woodshed, and cabin. I became fully alert at about the time the owls were waking and hit my writing stride on swing shift, from supper till one or two in the morning, working at a formica table by the light of propane lamps. This is more or less my pattern at home, unless I'm pressed into a more conventional schedule by legitimate work or some other aberration. I've always been a writer who sees his reflection in the midnight window and tries to peer through that image toward something more substantial beyond.

And I've always felt a mite defensive about it, as if writing in the company of darkness were somehow sleazy, questionable at best, particularly for someone identified as a nature writer. Well, to hell with that. My experiment settled the issue. For better or for worse I'm a night writer, at home or in the woods, and during my solitude I did some wondering about why it might be that I stay up half the night with the owls and moths and my pencil.

The most obvious influence of night is to limit what we can see and do, and for me this seems to foster the kind of introspective awareness in which creative work can grow. But I found during my solitude that darkness turned me outward, too. One evening early in my sojourn, I hiked home late from the river, happily burdened with two steelhead for the barbeque. Dusk turned to dark as I climbed the trail. I had my headlamp in necklace position, ready for use, but never turned it on. The trail, though indistinct, was clear enough. Where the forest opened slightly, I noticed a faint shadow moving alongside me, cast not by moon or stars but by the residual light of the thinly overcast sky. At the unlit cabin, after using the headlamp briefly to find down booties and a beer, I reclined in the La-Z-Boy chair and enjoyed, through a large window, the luminosity of early night, now with an evening planet in the west. Tall conifers stood around the meadow like a solemn council, their lower portions blended in shadow, their points and upper reaches sharply silhouetted against the sky. Somewhere among them a screech owl gave its tremulous call.

By day I could walk among those trees and note features of bark and foliage and habit that distinguish one species from another, and those that distinguish individuals within a species. I could call them by their common names — Douglas fir, white fir, sugar pine, ponderosa pine — and by their Latin names as well. But there is a blindness in that seeing. My vision catches on the surfaces of things, gets snagged and tugged about by their multiplicity. As I watched the trees in darkness it was not distinctions I saw but their commonality, not their names I knew them by but their essential namelessness. Backed by the planet's drop of liquid light and the first few stars, they announced their membership in a wilderness vaster than daylight eyes can apprehend, a wilderness to which I too belong. I felt closer to them. They seemed to have crept nearer.

———

Though I had no human neighbors, I did see human lights at night. Satellites—an alarming number—slipped silently among the stars, and once in a while a jetliner cruised high overhead, blinking its way with a whispery rumble. On certain moonless nights I saw in the southeast above Rattlesnake Ridge, the landform that dominated my view, a diffuse radiance—the luminous effluvium of several southern Oregon towns along Interstate 5, thirty to forty miles away. Twenty years ago there would have been less of a glow; fifty years ago, there would have been none. Our age is hostile to night and to all things dark—and so, paradoxically, we make night darker. As our human lights blaze brighter and reach farther, from within their field night looks blacker, and our estrangement only grows. Who can say what we are losing? Our kind, like other Earthly creatures, was born and came of age in the rhythmic recurrence of night and moon, the specked and clouded brilliance of the Milky Way. We saw the stars and somehow came to know that we were seeing them, came to fear, to hope, to wonder. Now, in this contemporary speck of evolutionary time, we wander in our own obliterating glare, lost—happily or wretchedly, but lost—in what we have made, progressively blinded to that which made us.

And not just in cities. On farms across the Midwest and Great Plains and on ranch after ranch throughout the American West, blaring mercury vapor lamps on tall poles come on automatically at dusk and shine boldly all night. Marketed as security lights, and no doubt useful from time to time, these beacons chiefly secure residents and visitors from any possibility of experiencing true night. One of my neighbors has two, which I am frequently tempted to shoot out, distant though they are. Yet I hoist myself by the same petard while camping, when I build a fire and stare into its lively lightedness for hours. And what am I but a perfect likeness of modern enlightened man when I hike or ski by headlamp, peering ahead in the bondage of my narrow lightbeam oblivious to the rest of the universe, accompanied at times by annoying moths just as monomaniacally addicted to light as I am?

Once in a while during my sojourn I would wake in the middle of the night and lie in bed a while, partly saturated with dream images, partly attentive to sounds — the patter of rain, a pop from the coals in the woodstove, a twig-snap from close by in the woods. At home I would probably distract myself with reading during such an interval, or my thoughts might turn busy and fretful. I might worry about getting back to sleep. In solitude I was more content simply to be; the most I'd think about would be the book I was writing, and usually I would merely drift with the night, my being astir with a sense of significance and sufficiency in my cosmos of nighted woods and starlight, and before too long I'd fall asleep again.

I wouldn't learn until four years later that my nocturnal wakenings replicated an ancient pattern. According to historian A. Roger Ekirch, pre-industrial Europeans and Americans tended to sleep in two shifts separated by an hour or more of spontaneous wakefulness. Ekirch has found references to "first sleep" (called also "dead sleep," probably reflecting the exhaustion of day laborers) in the writings of Chaucer, Plutarch, Virgil, and even as far back as Homer. The interval dividing first sleep from "second" or "morning" sleep was turned by some toward domestic attentions, in bed or out, but it seems that for many it passed in a state of mind something like what I experienced in solitude. Freed from daylight distractions, refreshed by a few hours' slumber, a man or woman could lie abed in a condition of easeful contemplation akin to meditation. Robert Louis Stevenson, who experienced the phenomenon intermittently, called it a "nightly resurrection" that freed him from the "Bastille of civilization."

Many animals sleep in multiple segments. It seems to be no anomaly but the norm of nature, and was for us until industrialization brought widespread artificial lighting. A study at the National Institute of Mental Health found that subjects deprived of (or freed from) artificial light at night developed a divided sleep pattern remarkably like that of earlier centuries. Ekirch quotes a chronobiologist as saying, "Every time we turn on a light we are inadvertently taking a drug that affects how we will sleep." It occurs to me that if I hadn't polluted my evenings in solitude with many hours of propane light, I might have reverted more completely to the segmented pattern.

It may make little difference whether our sleep is continuous or broken. But it also may be that in drenching ourselves in artificial light we have forfeited a unique way of belonging to darkness, through a fertile field of nighted consciousness that a medieval proverb characterized as the "mother of thoughtes." We may have lost one means of maintaining our mental and spiritual wholeness.

Reading a biography of Emerson during my solitude, I was reminded that in the nineteenth century it was common for inexpensive portraits to be drawn as silhouettes, the subject's head shown in profile as a sharply defined solid shadow. This practice waned with the advent of photographic techniques, but not everyone saw the change as an improvement. A photo, the critics argued, showed merely a particular moment; a silhouette was a timeless outline. The very fidelity of a photograph, its lit and focused precision, was felt to obscure the greater truth of spirit, which, though not directly observable, could be suggested by the silhouette.

Henry Thoreau, that quintessential morning person, also associated darkness with spirit. He took some of his rambles at night because he found it "necessary to see objects by moonlight as well as sunlight, to get a complete notion of them." Outside at dusk, he wrote in his *Journal*, "I begin to distinguish myself, who I am and where. . . . I recover some sanity. The intense light of the sun unfits me for meditation, makes me wander in my thoughts." In the dewy mist of a low-lying field, he reports, "I seem to be nearer the origin of things." And later, in open moonlight: "Our spiritual side takes a more distinct form, like our shadow which we see accompanying us."

Our spiritual side is of little interest to the lifestyle and reductive ideology of materialism. We believe in what we can clearly see and rap with our knuckles or measure with our keen and keener instruments, and spirit, after all, is unlikely to show up at a mall or under a microscope. It means *breath*, the life that breathes in all things, and it breathes in darkness as well as in light. St. John of the Cross, imprisoned for his heresies in a Spanish jail, wrote rapturously of night as the "sweet guider" that brought him closer to his God. The English metaphysical poet Henry Vaughan felt a similar intuition when he imagined the nature of God as "a deep but dazzling darkness":

> O for that night! where I in Him
> Might live invisible and dim!

Goethe and other German Romantics revived the expansive mystery of darkness in the head-heavy rationalism of the Enlightenment, and in America, as Thoreau was taking his moonlit walks, Walt Whitman sang of night's spirited beauties — "the mystic play of shadows twining and twisting as if they were alive" — in his long poem "Out of the Cradle Endlessly Rocking." In the twentieth century America found perhaps its greatest poet of night in Robinson Jeffers, who knew a sensuous, mysterious life abroad in the dark. "The splendor without rays," he called it, "the shining of shadow . . . Where the shore widens on the bay she opens dark wings / And the ocean accepts her glory."

In solitude I felt the presence of spirit on days when drifts and roils of mist moved slowly in the canyons of the Rogue and its tributaries. One green-fledged ridge or another would partially open to view and obscure again, open elsewhere along its length, then a different ridge would reveal a portion of itself, a ceaseless shifting of gray and green. Once I watched a great Douglas fir on a near ridge lapse repeatedly into mist and emerge distinct again in soft gray light, the same tree each time but each time freshly born, dewy with its own creation. The landscape seemed most alive, most in its element on those days. It had a gravitas, an aura of sentience, as if I had been allowed to see into the slow, secret life it withheld on days of brighter weather. A line of Emily Dickinson's kept recurring to me: "Nature spending with herself / Sequestered Afternoon. . . ." It was the paradox of that particular country, I came to see, that it most revealed itself when partially veiled.

In the short days of winter the sun sank behind the woods to the west as early as three-thirty. As the high, west-facing slope of Rattlesnake Ridge turned a deepening green-gold, a tinge of ghostliness came over my immediate surroundings of meadow and woods. The crisp shadows of afternoon dissolved, and in a progression without increments it seemed that their constituent darkness interfused the remaining light. Silence gathered with the dark, even as the river whispered louder from the bottom of the canyon. Apple trees, fence posts, deer in the meadow, all singular things withdrew into background, less and less present, insubstantial as fading memories. And then, with twilight, the council of trees, magnified in silhouette, monuments of a mystery I could not speak, but which the trees appeared to state quite clearly against the softly glowing sky.

We believe too confidently in eyesight. Through most of our doings we carry around us, like a snail its shell, a room veneered with that which is visible from moment to moment, and we tend to call that paneled room reality. But even in broad daylight, eyesight shows only a pittance of what is. As I hiked or fished or sat on the cabin deck, my vision gliding or hopping between features of woods or meadow or river or ridgelines, noticing this and noticing that, the real action was in the vast sectors of the unseen — the miles of fungal filaments in any ounce or two of forest soil, the prodigious traffic of food and fluids traveling the xylem and phloem of trees, the manifold borings and diggings and chewings and excretings of countless hidden insects, the even more arcane activities of bacteria and other tribes of the very small, the groundwater seeping inches a day along bedrock joints and aquifers of sand and gravel, and the far slower progress of tectonic uplift raising the Klamath Mountains as the Rogue and its tributary streams cut downward. . . . And those are only a few of the smaller mysteries, ones my mind can bring into focus. The universe, physicists say, seems to be mainly composed of a substance they call dark matter, invisible and so far undetectable. From the play of charmed sub-atomic particles to the reaches of interstellar space, Nature is largely a creature of mystery, a creature of darkness.

When I fished I couldn't see far into the sliding green current and lively riffles where I cast my line. As my lure throbbed against the current or bounced along the rocky and sandy bottom, I was feeling in the dark, trying to read braille, sometimes sensing a strike just before it occurred — the rod suddenly arched and thrumming with an unseen power thrusting this way and that, showing itself in glints and shadowed surges as I worked it nearer and finally, if I was lucky and it wasn't, raised it to the light of day where it didn't belong, a sleek iridescence flailing in my hands as I unhooked it. A few of the steelhead I caught I killed for meat, but it was the strike and play I fished for, the sudden calling of that wild energy awakening the same in me. Most of the fish went back to the river, their dark backs blending almost instantly into the opaque green depths.

Creative writing, like any art, is a kind of fishing. Poems and stories and essays arise from depths where the writer must feel for them in the dark. They rarely arise fully formed, but they never arise unformed at all. Like a fish on a line (often tenuously hooked), they manifest themselves in resistant glimpses — associations, bits of story, darts of feeling or idea — and the glimpses carry with them intimations of an order, an unseen wholeness they are part of. To realize that wholeness takes luck, patience, and usually a lengthy interplay between the headlamp of applied consciousness, which works the glimpses into provisional wordings, and the darkness beneath the surface — the deep river of the human psyche, fed by weathers of experience and springs of innate knowing, stirring with dreams, intuitive promptings, the murmured, insistent, half-heard urgings of spirit and soul.

An afternoon spent fishing seemed always to lead to a good night of writing, but most of my nights were good in any case. Whether I was in the cabin or out walking, the continuum of day-turning-night charged me, re-excited my interest in the work I would soon turn to with the lighting

LOOSE ON THE LAND

of the lamps. Little breaks outdoors—to watch Orion in the southern sky, or listen to rainfall on the covered deck, or howl into the canyon wondering if one could be conscious and truly wild as well—pepped me up as swing shift progressed and rounded the horn of midnight into graveyard. Maybe I need the company of darkness to stimulate my own darkness within, to excite its interest—or perhaps to excite my interest in it—or maybe it's just a matter of feeling at home. They are shy and tentative things, the stirrings that want life in words. You won't spot a mole in the light of sun, but at midnight, in the stillness of dark, he might just poke his nose above ground.

Ultimately I can't know why I write at night, and I don't need to know. The things of darkness belong to darkness. As X. J. Kennedy has written in a poem, when the goose got too curious about where her golden eggs came from, her head ended up in a dark and very unfortunate place. I do know that I want the lit particularities of the observed world in my writing. I want the jags and curves and rough or silky surfaces of material things, their hues and heft, the *exactly this* that they present. They save me from the futility of vagueness. But I also want in my writing the dimness of dusk, the shadowed hiding places of day, the silent swirl of a deep river pool; I want misted mountains and the light of stars and moon and the full dark of a new moon night. When I see little clear, I seem to see farther, deeper. Night saves me from the tyranny of appearances. In darkness I remember that it is not knowledge to which we most deeply belong but mystery, and I sense in the mystery of night a beauty exceeding even the great and notable beauties of the daylit world.

II

Oregon Rivers: A Suite in Six Parts

BEGINNINGS

The canyon is a vault of light, its streaked volcanic walls rising hundreds of feet above me. A prodigious job of excavation for a river as small and mild as this one, the West Little Owyhee, flowing at its October low among yellow and russet willows. An overhang of stone is reflected in the clear moving water, and water is reflected on the stone—a rippling, wavering river of light follows the river that follows the stone as it wears the stone away. The stream sings a subdued music, a scarcely audible lilt, faint and fluid syllables not quite said. It slips away into its future, where it already is, and flows steadily forth from up the canyon, a fountain of rumors from regions known to it and not to me.

We don't tend to ask where a lake comes from. It lies before us, contained and complete, tantalizing in its depth but not its origin. A river is a different kind of mystery, a mystery of distance and becoming, a mystery of source. Touch its fluent body and you touch far places. You touch a story that must end somewhere but cannot stop telling itself, a story that is always just beginning.

The West Little Owyhee starts somewhere in the vast sagebrush table-lands of far southeastern Oregon, maybe in a pocket of aspens dropping leaves into a pool that gives itself to a trickling over stones. Stories begin that way throughout the high desert country, on Steens Mountain and Hart Mountain, in the Trout Creeks and the Ochocos. And they begin, too, in dry rocky creases that wander the immense tablelands as if lost. They are not lost. When snow melts or enough rain falls they are the rivers gathering, finding their way, forming themselves as they gradually form the land.

In the Cascades and the Coast Range, the Wallowas and the Straw-berries, there are other kinds of beginnings. Spotting the forests are seeps and springs where grasses, mosses, and horsetails silently riot, growing and dying to grow and die and grow again. There are lakes surrounded by conifers or alpine meadow, lakes brimming full and overfull, pouring off through little ravines checked with boulders and beaver dams and the trunks of trees. Higher on the peaks there are slumping snowfields littered with rockfall, tinged pink with algae, the rubble below them glistening with melt. There are slow rivers of ice that hoard the story for centuries before letting it go in minuscule drops, in streamings milky with ground stone.

Start at any of those sources, let water lead you, and eventually you will stand where a river pours into the Pacific Ocean or a desert lake. The story isn't hard to follow. But start at the mouth and trace the story back, and your journey may involve more questions. Trace the Rogue River, to choose one. From its outlet at Gold Beach on the southern coast, follow it back through its wild canyon in the Klamath Mountains, through the broad valley it has formed between Grants Pass and Medford, and up past Lost Creek Reservoir into the Cascades. Climb alongside through the vol-canic landscape, where at one point the river hurls itself into a lava tube and churns out of sight for two hundred feet. Follow still higher, until the Rogue is nothing but a stream joined by other streams, all of them small and white and fast. You could follow any of them. *Here*, says the river, *here* and *here*.

Stay with the blue line your map calls the Rogue and you'll arrive, on foot, at a place called Boundary Springs, high in the northwest corner of Crater Lake National Park. But even here you'll face choices. There are several springs, each of them bright with moss and rushing water. Where is the Rogue River now? The largest spring? Take off your boots, douse your feet. Watch the lucid water spring forth among shaggy stones and cascade lightly away. Watch how it flows. It does not gather and then begin to move. It is born in motion, a gesture already underway. This spring is only the place where the story emerges from the deep cold joints of an exploded mountain, a subterranean wilderness of water fed by seepings out of Crater Lake, which itself is fed by underground springs, which themselves are fed by snowmelt seeping into soil.

Snowfall, then, is the source of the Rogue. But snow is only an expression of winter storms, and the storms are swirling eddies of a vast air mass that flows out of Siberia, soaks up moisture south of the Aleutians, and delivers barrages of weather to the West Coast. It is known as the Pacific maritime polar airstream, one of several such atmospheric tendencies that shape the North American climate. The headwaters of the Rogue, and the West Little Owyhee and every stream on Earth, is a river in the sky.

No one in the ancient world would have been surprised by such an idea, but the ancients knew their rivers in the sky through myth, not atmospheric science. The early Greeks imagined a divine river as the god Okeanos, who encircled the universe and coupled with his wife and sister, Tethys, to produce the three thousand earthly rivers. The Egyptians believed that not one but two Niles flowed through their world — the great river of water whose floods fertilized their fields, and a celestial Nile that rose from the same source and tended across the heavens. By day the celestial river bore the boat of Ra the Sun; at night it shone and glittered as the Milky Way.

As civilization evolved in the Ganges Valley of India, it was believed that a heavenly river identified with the goddess Shakti poured down upon the head of Shiva, who eased the torrential power of her waters and sent them streaming to the four directions. The southern branch became the Ganges, which to Hindus is more than sacred — it is divinity itself in liquid manifestation. Bathing in the Ganges, polluted as it may be, purifies one's present life and past lives of sin; pilgrims take home bottles of its water for healing.

The Book of Genesis gives a brief glimpse of that same archetypal river: "And a river went out of Eden to water the garden, and from thence it was parted, and became into four heads." Ezekiel envisions the waters of life as a small trickle issuing from the threshold of the Jerusalem Temple. As the Lord leads him downstream, the waters rise to his ankles, his knees, his loins, and finally they swell into a mighty river lined on both sides with fruitful and medicinal trees.

Almost all mythic cosmogonies begin with water. It is the primeval element, "the face of the deep," the formless potential that pre-exists the created world and sustains its being. "Water flows," wrote religious historian Mircea Eliade, "it inspires, it heals, it prophesies. By their very nature, spring and river display power, life, perpetual renewal; they *are* and they are *alive.*"

In Greek mythology the splash and stir of water came to be personified in the nymphs, female divinities of birth and fertility who cured the sick and raised mortal children to be heroes. Nymphs remained forever beautiful and young. They were sometimes oracles, and oracles in general were associated with springs and streams — perhaps because of the inherent mystery in water issuing from the ground, or because water in motion sometimes seems to utter an elusive speech. Before responding to questions, oracles drank from the waters, often in a cave. Through them the mystery of living water expressed itself to the minds of men.

Like the oracle's news, however, the gifts of water were not always benign. An ancient Syrian statue of the Great Mother shows her gowned in a river flowing from a vase she holds, fish swimming upward in its current. But the goddess appears in other images with demonic eyes, lightning jagging from her brow. On the Nile, the Indus, the Tigris and Euphrates, the giver of life was sometimes a destroyer, withholding her fertility and canceling human lives through drought or flood. Even the nurturing nymphs were feared by the Greeks as thieves of children, and in midday heat they were capable of dissolving mortals in madness and drawing them to doom in the rushing waters. Through such ideas the ancients acknowledged that water is a wild power, ungovernable, containable only by paradox. Its nature is to give birth and to ruin, to sustain the things of creation and claim them to itself again.

That dual nature is central to the rite of baptism, which is at once a death—a disintegration of one's old identity—and a birth, a pouring forth of the divine into one's mortal life. Baptism was originally a ritual of flowing water specifically, water in its living movement. In Egypt, purification by water was associated with Osiris and Isis, god and goddess of the rising and falling Nile. In Hindu tradition, water must be set in motion by pouring from a vessel when no stream or river is available. Among Jews before the time of Christ, baptism was accomplished by immersing the naked boy in a flowing stream seven days after circumcision. Ritual pools were used as well, but John the Baptist shunned those and performed his rites in the River Jordan, long known for its healing power. It was in the Jordan that John baptized the one who came after him, and when Christ emerged from the river's current, "he saw the Spirit of God descending like a dove, and lighting upon him."

Many early Christians continued to baptize in John's way, as did Gnostic peoples such as the Mandaeans in what are now Iran and Iraq. "Be baptized with the flowing water I have brought you from the world of light," it is written in their *Right Ginza*. "Clothe yourselves in white, to be like the mystery of this flowing water." In the modern world, pouring water from a baptismal font or dunking in a pool are more common than immersion in a stream, but the symbolism of baptism remains powerful. Living water is the gesture from beyond. It returns us to beginnings and makes us anew. It joins the timeless to the temporal, the sacred to the secular, the heavenly to the mundane.

But if flowing water is a thoroughfare connecting those realms, it is also, ever paradoxical, the line of demarcation between them. Perhaps because rivers, aside from seashores, form the clearest boundaries found in nature, the crossing of a river became the human psyche's primary symbol for the passage of death. Beyond the earthly Jordan lies the promised land; beyond the spiritual Jordan lies the promised land of heaven. The Greeks buried their dead with a coin in the mouth for Charon, the grumpy boatman who ferried souls across the River Acheron to the realms of Hades.

The Babylonians had a similar notion, and the theme occurs in both the Shinto and Buddhist traditions of Japan. (One of the ancient meanings of nirvana is "the far shore.") Among Hindus, holy sites are known as *tirthas*—fords—because they are considered propitious places to make the crossing from this earthly world of illusion. It was inevitable that Herman Hesse's Siddhartha should come to a river near the end of his life of seeking. He lived out his days as a ferryman, poling travelers on their necessary journeys as he meditated on the river, listened to its voices, and heard in it at last all laughter and all sorrow, the flowing wholeness he had yearned for all his life.

When we cross the Willamette on one of the bridges in Portland or Eugene or Salem, we don't see it as a mythic being. We don't toss handfuls of grass as a sacrifice, as do the Masai of East Africa when they cross their rivers. Looking down on the workaday river with its boats and barges, its riprapped banks, we aren't likely to think of it as sacred or alive, a gesture from another world. We aren't moved to perform baptisms in it. We of the modern world have sought other kinds of value in our rivers. We have subdued them and turned them into channels of commerce. We have diverted them to water our fields, loaded them with sewage, torn up their beds and banks for gold and gravel, blockaded them to control their floods and extract their energy, stripped and muddied their basins for timber and pasture, poisoned them with industrial wastes, and reduced their abounding runs of wild anadromous fish to fractional remnants.

We have treated rivers as convenient perpetual motion machines, mere volumes of useful water and energy, yet even our tightly harnessed industrial rivers still beckon us. Whatever we have done to them, a mystery still flows before us. Like ocean watchers, we walk and rest beside our rivers, gazing, listening, drifting. When the docile waters rise, we flock to see the wildness in them, the wrack and foam, the intent sweeping power. Despite the damage floods can do, it reassures us in our depths to know, with Wordsworth, that "The river glideth at his own sweet will."

All of us have touched and been touched by flowing water. Our ancestors have eaten and loved and raised children by rivers for as long as we have been human, and longer. We have known the music of living water for the entire evolutionary saga of our coming of age on Earth. "It seems to flow through my very bones," writes Henry Thoreau of a brook he knew. "What is it that I hear but the pure waterfalls within me, in the circulation of my blood, the streams that fall into my heart?"

Spiritually we understand rivers far less well than the ancients did, but even in the rational light of our science the creative and destructive nature of running water remains wonderful enough. We know that it began its Earthly work as soon as rains first fell and traveled the face of the young volcanic planet, and if not for continual tectonic uplift, it would long ago have erased the continents into a global sea. Through that tireless attrition, that primordial youthful energy, water carves out rills, runnels, clefts, ravines, hollows, valleys, chasms, canyons — the intricate inworn branching of watersheds, the aging face of the land, the very places that we know as home. And in that webwork of water, in and around and gathered together by its flexuous body, a labyrinthine ecology connects our human lives to the least and greatest of the lives around us, an ecology we are only beginning to fathom and are unlikely ever to comprehend in its wholeness.

And, of course, we are connected historically to rivers. They led Euro-Americans into the continent and eventually across it, showing the way into the Oregon Country for Lewis and Clark, for trappers and missionaries, for the pioneers of the Oregon Trail. Columbia, McKenzie, Illinois, John Day, Sprague, Deschutes, Powder, Malheur, Long Tom, Rogue — you can hear the history in the names, you can glimpse the stories we have spun around rivers. But listen to more: Klamath, Imnaha, Sycan, Umpqua, Elk, Salmon, Snake, Wenaha, Wallowa, Clackamas, Nestucca, Chewaucan. There are other and older histories here, interwoven with the flowing of rivers for thousands of years before Europeans set foot on the North American continent. And there are hints in those names of a still more ancient time, traces of a primeval vitality, echoes of original voices sounding in the land before any human being was alive to hear or name them.

The subdued autumnal music of the West Little Owyhee, flowing now in starlight beside my camp, is one such voice. There are many more. The Snake, where this mild water is bound, surges through Hells Canyon with the power of the Rocky Mountains behind it. The two Indian Creeks on Steens Mountain tumble down aspen-flagged valleys to the Donner und Blitzen. The White River flings itself from Mount Hood's shoulders; the Metolius wends its stately way among ponderosa pines; the Chetco, rising in the rugged Kalmiopsis, incises steep canyons down to the sea. The Oregon land is alive with waters. Where we haven't choked them of their voices the rivers still sound, their fountains spring forth from the world of light, they pursue the blind and beautiful labor of time.

Water Ways

Oregon's mountains are mostly immigrants. The Blues and the Klamaths have been here longest, scraped onto the western flank of early North America from the back of a drifting tectonic plate about a hundred and twenty million years ago. Catty-cornered now, a state apart, the two ranges then sat side by side, two island clumps in the deep sea that was Oregon. Much of the state's land mass arrived the same way, in a series of migrations from the near and far Pacific. The foundation of the Coast Range may have been the most recent arrival, but more likely was formed in a series of volcanic eruptions close offshore. Eventually our state gained fifty miles as the North American plate, under pressure from the Juan de Fuca plate plunging one inch per year beneath it, buckled and folded upward as the Coast Range uplands, brief rivers dissecting the mild heights. Eastward the crust subsided into the trough of the Willamette Valley, which was not created by the river.

The subducting Juan de Fuca raises periodic seismic and volcanic fits as it melts into Earth's mantle. The Cascades were born in several such episodes, mounds of ash and lava tilting up to the east as streams wore furrowed flowlines into them. Still farther east, the crust of Earth stretched tectonically, vastly increasing itself, slipping into basins between fault block mountains. Beginning some seventeen million years ago, that movement gave vent to stupendous lava flows that may have spread as fast as thirty miles per hour, creating in the course of several million years the Columbia Plateau, one of the largest flood basalt provinces in the world, thousands of feet deep. As flow after flow poured through the wide gap that preceded the Columbia River Gorge, the Columbia persistently shifted its channel northward, cutting around each new deposit of basalt.

In Pleistocene times, beginning two million years ago, ice sheets covered the High Cascades, the Wallowas, the Elkhorns, and the Strawberries, carving peaks into rocky horns, plowing broad sloping valleys down Steens Mountain. Glaciers flowed where streams had flowed before them; when the ice receded, streams flowed again in the greater valleys. The ice withdrew most recently about fifteen thousand years ago, leaving vast lakes in the lowlands, small lakes in the mountains. A lake is usually one of two things: a puddle left by a river of ice, or a river of water temporarily blocked by a moraine, slide, ice dam, lava flow, or humanly constructed dam. None of them last very long. In a geological film of Oregon, shot from the sky at one frame per century, lakes would be seen to come and go like transient spatters of rain. Rivers would shift their channels from side to side, their meanders traveling downstream, but they would largely persist, largely hold their courses. The present channel may be young; the drainage pattern is very old.

There was a Columbia River before there was a Cascade Range. As the mountains upwarped, the river cut down and kept pace. In a similar way, the Rogue and Umpqua have downcut through the rapid uplift of the Klamath Mountains and the Coast Range, respectively; of the rivers originating in the Cascades, only those two achieve a direct Oregon outlet to the sea. The Klamath, remarkably enough, rises east of the Cascades and incises its way through that range and the Klamath Mountains as well to reach its outlet on the northern California coast.

Farther east in Oregon, the main stem of the Owyhee has been flowing in its present channel for upwards of five million years, adjusting all the while to volcanic eruptions, the stretch and tilting of the lively crust. The Metolius predates Black Butte, the volcano under which it now seeps, emerging in three great springs near the butte's northern base. The Deschutes has been slicing Columbia Plateau basalts for four to five million years, downcutting two to three thousand feet in that time. More recent lavas, from the Newberry vents, filled its canyon—and those of the Crooked and Metolius—eight hundred feet deep. The rivers reclaimed their canyons in a mere one million years, eating into the cold stone, reducing it to lava islands and high streamside cliffs.

But rivers do die. They dry up, they are interred beneath miles of lava, and sometimes they devour one another. The present Snake River is thought to be a young cannibal. One of its Pliocene headwater streams came from the vicinity of a tight oxbow the river now makes as it flows northward into Hells Canyon. An older and much larger river system tended southwesterly through the same area, ponding up in ancient Lake Idaho. As the Snake River Plain tilted northward, the young Snake wore through a divide, drained the lake, and captured the greater river's current, suddenly adding hundreds of miles and the snows of Yellowstone to its watershed. The decapitated river was left to dry and fill, a geologic ghost.

The Pleistocene was an eventful epoch for the Northwest, particularly the period from sixteen to fourteen thousand years ago—a scant second, by the timekeeping of geologists. Lake Missoula, in what is now western Montana, rose to a depth of nearly two thousand feet and an area of three thousand square miles when a lobe of the Cordilleran ice sheet plugged the canyon of the Clark Fork River. Periodically the ice gave way, releasing five hundred cubic miles of water to surge across eastern Washington at speeds comparable to cars on a freeway. The deluge channeled into the Columbia at Wallula Gap, surged eight hundred feet deep or more when it hit the narrows of the Columbia Gorge—which it thoroughly reamed out, though the gorge's tall waterfalls already existed—then backed up again on the lower Columbia, drowning the present site of Portland under four hundred feet of water and inundating the Willamette Valley nearly to the present site of Eugene. The lake probably persisted for weeks, a muddy roil tossing icebergs and torn-out trees. Boulders from Montana were stranded around the valley, borne in by rafts of ice.

Those erratics and other evidence, including Washington's great coulees and Montana gravels deposited high in the Columbia Gorge, made sense to no one except a lone geologist named J Harlen Bretz (he eschewed the period after his initial), who announced the flood theory in 1923 and defended it for decades against a disbelieving profession. The clincher came when a series of long parallel hills in Montana were identified from an airplane as what they are: ripple marks left by the second greatest series of floods in Earth's known geologic record. (The greatest occurred in what is now Russia.) The Cordilleran ice lobe regularly gave way and reformed, releasing as many as forty to fifty Ice Age floods. Among their many consequences are the rich Willamette silts, tens to hundreds of feet deep, from which farmers raise corn, berries, and grass seed today.

Parts of the story of rivers are best told in numbers.

Over ninety-seven percent of all water on Earth is in the oceans. Ice caps and glaciers hold just upwards of two percent. Most of the slight remainder, six-tenths of one percent, occurs as groundwater, ranging from the top of the water table to a depth of three miles. A smidgen, seventeen one-thousandths of one percent, can be found in lakes. A smaller smidgen, one one-thousandth of one percent, circulates as vapor in the atmosphere, to an altitude of seven miles. By far the smallest fraction of the world's water, at any one moment only one ten-thousandth of one percent, flows in rivers and streams. A negligible quantity, but without that tiny portion of water in motion the face of our planet would be the face of a stranger.

Strangely, though, it has been generally realized for only two centuries that flowing water shapes the land at all. Aristotle, Leonardo, and others throughout history have understood erosion, but the prevailing view through the Middle Ages and well into the Enlightenment held that valleys pre-existed their streams. They were thought to be effects of the Biblical flood or of natural catastrophe. Knowledge of the Bretz floods in North America would have aided that view, had it been available, but landscape in the long run changes very gradually. Catastrophism has released its hold on the human mind slowly, like rock giving way to a river.

And where did the water of streams and rivers come from? That mystery also persisted for centuries. The ancients could see that rain and snow augmented streams, but not enough fell, it seemed, to account for year-round flow. If the ancients had lived in western Oregon they might have figured it out, but they believed that Okeanos, the world-encircling river, penetrated underground and rose, purified of its salt, in springs and streams. Scientific understanding of the hydrologic cycle didn't come into focus until the seventeenth century, when a Frenchman measured rainfall in the Seine basin and found it six times adequate to account for the river's discharge. It was left for the astronomer Edmond Halley to complete the cycle by identifying evaporation as the origin of precipitation.

In the course of a year, a full three feet of water evaporates from the world's oceans. Nine-tenths of it falls directly back to its source; one-tenth falls on land as rain or snow. A molecule of that land precipitation that runs off into a stream is likely to be in the ocean again within a few weeks or days, or it may return to the atmosphere, more quickly yet, through evaporation. Other routes are slower. The molecule may spend decades in a lake, centuries in a glacier. If it enters the soil, and isn't sucked into a plant and transpired, it might percolate through the semisaturated surface zone toward the nearest lake or river. Or it might descend to the water table, the zone of saturation in which every crack and pore is packed with water, and travel there an inch or two a day through aquifers of sand or gravel, of fractured or porous rock. If the molecule sinks deeper than half a mile, it is likely to join rain that fell ten thousand years ago and will return to the hydrologic cycle only if and when a tectonic disturbance releases it. Deeper yet, hot from the radioactive decay of Earth's core and loaded with dissolved salts, lies water that left the cycle millions of years ago. And still deeper, bound up in crystalline rocks, there exists water that has never flowed, water that was present in the spinning dust from which the solar system formed.

But rivers care nothing for those deep places. Rivers are children of sky and upper Earth, deft and lively, born from rain and snowmelt fed into their channels by steady seepage from the zone of saturation. That seepage provides the river's base flow, its minimum year-round level. When rain swells the base flow, by surface runoff and percolation through the banks, there is an increase in the river's discharge — the volume of water per second passing a particular point. Rivers are self-adjusting organisms, and so any change in discharge must be answered by changes in other dimensions: mainly, channel width, channel depth, and velocity of flow. In small streams of upper drainage regions, increased discharge results primarily in higher velocity, with a small increase in channel depth. In lower regions, along the river's floodplain, discharge is inherently greater due to continual contributions of seepage and tributaries along the way, and the effects of storm contributions are magnified. This heightened discharge is accommodated by a downstream expansion of channel width, a lesser increase in depth, and often — surprisingly — a higher velocity than occurs in the river's mountain origins.

How can a flatter stretch of river flow faster than a much steeper stretch? Because gradient is not the only determinant of velocity. The loss in gradient is more than compensated by the enlarged river's greater discharge, and by two factors that reduce frictional drag: the smoothness of the downstream bed, which is typically more sandy than rocky, and the fact that as the river grows in volume, the portion of its flow in contact with its bed and banks grows proportionately smaller. High in the Cascades, the little Rogue River tumbles down steep slopes but tumbles inefficiently, squandering much of its energy as it dashes among rocks and fallen trees. Close to its mouth, two hundred miles downriver, it flows at a milder pitch but flows evenly, massively, with gathered and concerted power, along its smooth sandy bed.

But even that smoother reach of river flows evenly only in a relative sense. A river never moves at uniform speed across a transect of its flow. In a smooth artificial channel, and perhaps for brief passages in very even natural channels, the current may exhibit laminar flow: the water glides in stable layers shearing one atop another. But the riverbeds of nature are variously irregular, creating complexity of movement. Water progresses downstream chaotically, with backflows and eddies, upflows and downflows, velocity pulsations, rollers, whirlpools, and standing waves. It is a continuous dance of turbulence, slackening only in a thin boundary layer near banks and bed, where velocity decreases to a theoretic zero.

Within that dance another goes on. A water molecule is an electrically dipolar structure, its two hydrogen atoms forming a positive pole and its oxygen atom a negative pole, causing the unbalanced molecules to attract each other like tiny magnets. This hydrogen bond, as it is known, makes water cling together at the molecular level in a cohesive continuity, bound more tightly than the molecules of some metals. As ice, the molecules are held in a set matrix; in the fluid state, the hydrogen bonds loosen enough for the molecules to swirl liquidly in constant motion, small bands of them bonding and unbonding willy-nilly in an ongoing submicroscopic frolic. The upshot, to our senses, is a substance that can resist no stress and therefore cannot hold still, that is easily parted by anything solid but as easily rejoins itself and dances on.

When water wets soil or rock (or a drinking glass, for that matter), some of its molecules form hydrogen bonds with the molecular constituents of those materials. It is this capacity, together with the acids it carries, that makes water a nearly universal solvent and thus the powerful agent of weathering and erosion that it is. Physical force is also erosive—a wind-driven drop of rain actually blasts tiny shards out of rock of any hardness. The aggregate effect of those little explosions and dissolutions is the reduction of the North American continent by about one foot every ten thousand years. Water loosens it, bit by bit, and water bears it away. To earth scientists, a stream is not a dancer but a worker, and its work consists of carrying its load—a dissolved load of rock and soil constituents, a suspended load of sand and other small particulates, and a bed load of gravel and larger stones that roll and bounce and slide along the bottom during high flows.

Like width, depth, and velocity, a river's capacity to carry its load varies with discharge. Peak flow events can scour the channel deeper by several feet, then rebuild it as discharge drops and the current loses its capacity. Differential current speeds sort the load as it's released, commonly producing an alternating pattern of pools (deep areas of slow current bedded with fine particles) and riffles (shallow stretches of livelier current and a gravel and cobble bed). Like the river itself, a riffle bed is both transient and permanent; it receives stones from upstream and loses stones downstream, the structure holding its place. Riffles alternate side to side in the channel, and consistently, in streams of all sizes, they occur at a distance of five to seven channel-widths apart. No one knows why.

In a straight reach, a river's fastest flowline tends to run in the center of the stream, just below the surface (because the atmosphere exerts a minute friction), but in most rivers most of the time the fastest flowline will swing from bank to bank with the curving of the channel. As the current presses into the outside of a bend, it piles slightly from centrifugal force and plunges strongly downward, eroding the bank and bottom, then rises as it crosses the center of the channel to surge against the outer bank of the next, opposite bend. And so the river body as a whole spirals down its channel, a helical dynamo carving pools at its outside bends, depositing the eroded material in riffles and bars along the inside bends, all of which amplifies the bending process itself.

Sinuosity is the lovely term for the windingness of rivers — or, if you prefer Greek to Latin, meandering. (The word comes from the river Maeander in Asia Minor, known anciently for its curving habit.) It used to be taught that meandering is characteristic of aged rivers, something like the aimlessness of a senile mind, and it is true that a lowland river in a broad valley will meander widely across its floodplain. But in fact all rivers meander, if permitted by their underlying geology. Straight reaches more than ten channel-widths in length are extremely rare, and even in a straight reach the deepest part of the channel will swing from side to side. Using laboratory flumes and various bed materials, researchers have watched sinuosity develop in a stream of constant discharge flowing in a perfectly straight channel. Local erosion gives the stream a small bed load, which it transports a short distance and deposits along the same bank it came from. Thus a slight bend is born, helical flow develops, and the initial bend propagates others downstream as the current increasingly deflects from bank to bank.

Such studies notwithstanding, there is as yet no entirely satisfactory theory explaining why rivers meander, and the mystery is not limited to rivers. All flowing water is sinuous — ocean currents, trickles over smooth stones, the raindrops coursing down your windshield. Water takes a winding way. Small streams wind small, big rivers wind big; mapped and brought into scale with each other, their sinuosity looks exactly the same. The wavelength of a stream's meanders — the straight-line distance between the apex of one bend and the apex of the next similar bend — will almost always equal seven to ten channel-widths. No one can account for this regularity. It seems to reflect a primary natural law, some original pact that water made with gravity and the solid matter of the world.

The ghostly mathematics of running water extends to the structure of watersheds, which tend to be dendritic, or treelike. Tributaries grow like branches, elongating at the tips and bifurcating as the drainage pattern impresses itself into the land. The twig-tips are categorized by geomorphologists as first-order streams — those with no tributaries. The stream formed by two first-order streams is second-order; two of those converging yield a third-order stream, and on up the ranks. (On the ground, a first-order stream is a hard creature to identify. Small permanent streams are fed by intermittent streams, which are fed by transient rills, which merge upslope with the planar landscape. In practice, a river's order depends on the scale of the map used to examine the watershed. By one analysis, the Willamette is an eighth- or ninth-order river, and the Columbia is twelfth-order.)

In any dendritic watershed, a stream of a given order is very likely to have either three or four tributaries of the next-lower order. A fifth-order stream, for example, will have three or four fourth-order tributaries, and each of those will be fed by three or four third-order tributaries, and so on. Further, each lower-order stream will be about half the length of the higher-order stream it feeds, and each will drain about one-fifth the area drained by the larger stream. The network shapes itself in a proportionate pattern, and that pattern holds roughly true in watersheds at any scale, from the tiny tracks of rainwater on a sloping desert stone to the enormous drainage of the Amazon, the greatest on Earth.

A dendritic network is the most efficient means of draining a slope; it requires less total length of channel than would, say, a network of parallel, non-branching tributaries. It can be predicted that a watershed will form dendritically, unless prevented by obdurate geology, but it can't be predicted exactly where the branching channels will form, how the pattern will arrange itself in any one instance. The pattern occurs but is not imposed; it is formed by the very flow of energy and mass it organizes. Networks of roots or neurons or blood vessels develop the same way—the general pattern determined, the particular realization singular. Schematically, those networks are very hard to distinguish from the network of a watershed. The dendritic form seems to be an archetype of nature, integral to the very being and becoming of things. Some geomorphologists have taken to calling it "the fingerprint of God." When Thoreau wrote of waterfalls in the circulation of his blood, of streams flowing into his heart, his imagination touched a pattern that unites us deeply with the patterned world around us.

LIFE AMONG THE RUINS

"Rivers," hydrologist Luna Leopold wrote, "are gutters down which flow the ruins of continents." His definition is fine as far as it goes, but a lot more than the transport of eroded material occurs in those gutters. If rivers run with entropic inevitability, life in rivers constitutes an ongoing stay of the inevitable. The hydrologic river works most efficiently unchecked. The ecologic river makes the most of every check along its course, setting its creatures stubbornly in place with adaptive forms and behaviors, mounting an elaborate and ingenious resistance from within the very grasp of almighty gravity.

Sinuosity aids the biologic conspiracy. If rivers ran straight they would offer an inauspicious sameness of habitat, not to mention fiercer currents. Meanders generate pools, riffles, eddies, bars, a varied and shifting mosaic of bed materials and current speeds and sun exposures. The exploitation of those variances is canny and complete. Pools, for example, are erosional features par excellence — sites scooped out and scoured at high water, signs of the gutter working at its violent best. But those same pools, at lower water, are the stream's richest havens of life. A pool is a hedge against quick export of the organic material — leaves, needles, twigs, feces, dead organisms — that provides fuel for stream food webs. In a well-pooled stream, organic matter is released only after thorough processing reduces it to fine particles and dissolved carbon. Ecologic efficiency thrives on retention.

Pools are structures inherent to the geomorphology of streams, but they are also created by objects and forces from outside the stream. In

Oregon watersheds before Euro-American settlement, great numbers of big trees fell into streams and rivers. Fallen trees structured much of the total channel length of streams up to fourth-order, yielding a characteristic stairstep pattern of flat pools behind debris dams and plunge pools below them. The fallen trees themselves became habitat and food for various invertebrates, including some of the longest-lived insects known to science, and the pools they formed were essential rearing sites for young trout and salmon, providing ample food and protection from swift currents.

In larger streams, fifth-order and higher, fallen trees rarely formed complete dams but did contribute to the formation of braided channel systems, with bars and quiet backwaters where young fish and waterfowl could thrive. High flows shifted and reconfigured the wood debris, intricating the river into an ever-changing complexity of structure and habitat. As late as 1870 the Willamette River flowed in at least five channels between Eugene and Corvallis, its floodplain cloaked with half a mile of forest on each side. Over a ten-year period on one fifty-mile stretch of the river, more than five thousand drift trees were removed from the channel for reasons of commerce and recreation—trees up to nine feet in diameter and a hundred and twenty feet long.

Drift trees of that size and larger once entered the Pacific in droves, the normal attrition of healthy, rivered forests. Most of them stranded on the coast, but some caught an offshore current and rafted westward, high seas emissaries from the old-growth watersheds of the Pacific Northwest. Much of the driftwood on the Hawaiian Islands derives from the West Coast of North America. Ancient Hawaiian cultures prized Douglas fir above all, crafting it into double canoes that carried their chieftains. In the course of their Pacific odyssey, trees and rafts of trees became, with the shade they cast, nuclei of marine food webs involving plankton, small fish, tuna, and porpoises. And at least one animal resident of Northwest streams, the humble water strider, became a North Pacific seafarer, living and propagating on the woody flotsam of its home forests.

This aboriginal mode of log export has drastically diminished in the last hundred years, as old-growth forests have been clearcut and river channels improved. And beaver dams, another principal means by which stream waters were detained—especially important east of the Cascades, where sparser forests contribute fewer debris dams—are also much rarer now. Those most industriously American of animals (European beaver don't build dams) once transformed waterways into stable chains of ponds and wetlands where food webs prospered. Almost half a million beaver were trapped out of Oregon and southwest Washington during one four-year period in the 1830s; by 1900 the species was close to extinction in this region. As the dams washed out, streams began to run unchecked, incising their channels and separating themselves from their floodplains.

The genius of a floodplain is that it takes on storm flows and diffuses their power. Water rushing in the channel loses much of its energy when it overtops its banks, and riparian vegetation—willows, cottonwoods, various shrubs and herbs—further restrains it, filtering sediment and fertile biomass from the flow. A river is an equilibrium between channel and floodplain, erosion and deposition; a river that can't get to its floodplain can only erode. The characteristic look of the lower reaches of the Sprague, the Malheur, the John Day, and many other dryland streams—incised channel, raw cutbanks, poor streamside vegetation—is the result of many impacts, including more than a century of grazing and logging. But their decline was set in motion before a single wagon had traveled the Oregon Trail, by traders of the North West and Hudson's Bay companies responding to a craze for black beaver top hats in the capitals of Europe.

By one estimate, Oregon's beaver population may stand at about one-tenth its ancestral level. In some extensively clearcut regions of the state, the animals are coming back—beaver are fond of willow, young alder, salmonberry, and other plants that return quickly to logged-over riparian zones—but their dams are relatively few, just as dams formed by fallen trees are far fewer than they were. Most watersheds in the Cascades and Coast Range have been stripped of sizable wood; their streams have lost their most important structural element. A recent re-survey of Columbia Basin streams first studied in the 1930s shows an average deep pool loss, outside of wilderness areas, of seventy-five percent. Fewer pools mean fewer fish, impoverished ecosystems. Unchecked flow means faster down-cutting, more sediment movement. The streams still flow, and many of them still look beautiful, but the landscape is losing its margin, its resilience, its capacity to absorb change. Slowly, and not so slowly, the landscape loses its life.

It's hard to make a living in a river under the best of circumstances. Most organisms manage by anchoring themselves to the bed material or obstructions in the channel. A boulder in the current forms an eddy on its downstream side, a refuge for various creatures, and its nooks and crevices and protected undersurface offer additional niches. Cobbles, gravel, even grains of sand provide exploitable substrates suited to different forms of life. Plants of all kinds are used for shelter as well as for food. And beneath the river's bed and banks, in the saturated zone where water moves downstream much more slowly, invertebrates that do not live in the channel can be found, some of them unpigmented and blind.

Most surfaces receiving light in a stream will be blanketed by tiny forests of periphyton, a diverse assemblage of algae, euglenoids, and bacteria that grows in crusted, stalked, filamentous, and gelatinous forms and varies through the seasons. Each population is adapted to the flow regime of its reach of river. Some species of algae, for instance, will grow erect in colonial forms in easy currents, prostrate and in crevices in faster water. Periphyton attaches to its substrate with specialized basal cells or glues itself with basal mucilage.

The periphyton mat is cropped by various grazing invertebrates. Snails often dominate the headwaters of Oregon streams, plowing through the miniature forests and scraping them up with raspy tongues. Black fly larvae graze for part of their life cycle, but also, taking advantage of the current they must resist, attach themselves to stones and filter fine particulate matter from the stream flow. The larva, anchored at its base, leans far back into the current with two feathery fans extending from its head, one sometimes held lower than the other to catch drift passing at different levels. Caddisfly larvae spin silky nets and make protective cases for themselves by embedding sand, pebbles, and bits of stick into a tube of silk. They are acutely adapted to nuances of current—one species will be found on a rock's upper surface in the fastest flow, another lower down in the intermediate zone, still another on sheltered undersurfaces.

Adaptive body forms and behaviors enable many creatures to stay put. The water-penny, a kind of beetle, looks like a completely flattened pill bug; it clings fast to stones with the help of tiny spines ringing its oval body. Tadpoles in rapid streams are equipped with a hydraulic sucker that allows them to hold on to stones for stability. (One ecologist reports that pebbles five times the tadpole's weight can be lifted using the tadpole as a handle.) Baetid mayfly nymphs have perfectly streamlined bodies, widest one-third of the way from the head; the long tapered abdomen swings freely like a weathervane, orienting the nymph directly into shifting microcurrents. Trout and salmon are shaped similarly, blunt in front and tapered behind, the form that best reduces turbulent drag created when an object separates the flow of current.

Salmon protect their eggs from current and predators by depositing them into gravel pits, called redds, the female makes by flapping her tail as she lies on her side. After the hovering male ejects his milt, the female excavates a new pit just upstream and the gravel she displaces covers the eggs just fertilized. Certain minnows take more extreme measures. They place their eggs in a cleared pit, like salmon, but then the male heaps gravel over them in a pile as high as twelve inches and as wide as three feet, carrying the pebbles in his mouth. To create this structure, one three-inch minnow may swim a total distance of fifteen miles carrying an aggregate underwater weight of eighty-eight pounds.

Reduced to a mouthful, the story of animals living in rivers is this: small ones cling to rock and wood, big ones eat small ones who have lost their grip. Not surprisingly, there is a continuous background level of small organisms — mostly insects, crustaceans, and snails — flushed downstream at the mercy of the current. This phenomenon is known as the drift. For reasons not entirely understood, the population of the drift jumps sharply, often by an order of magnitude, shortly after dark. This mass nocturnal movement may be evidence of an adaptive strategy whereby invertebrates find new feeding sites, or relief from fractious brethren or overcrowded conditions, while protected by darkness from the mouths of predators. Like Huck Finn, they give themselves to the river, traveling by night. Vast quantities of creatures are involved in the drift. An enterprising researcher once bulldozed a hundred and sixty yards of a Swedish river to clear it of all fauna, then measured the repopulation by drift. After eleven days he found up to seventy-four hundred invertebrates per square yard, which for the whole stretch of river extrapolates to a pioneering influx of four million tiny animals with a biomass of about ten pounds.

In broad ecological terms, the drift may simply be a system's way of sloughing off the excess above its carrying capacity. But with a continuous and very substantial removal of organisms down the gutter, how do populations maintain themselves? Why aren't headwaters and upper reaches depleted? It seems that compensating behaviors have evolved. Mayflies, stoneflies, and many other insects characteristically fly upstream to lay their eggs, and some insects migrate upstream in both their aquatic and aerial stages. Trout generally swim upstream to spawn. Nearly all riverine animals instinctively face into the current, and so to move at all means initially to move upstream. Snails have been observed to travel upriver, maybe as far as one mile in a year. *Gammurus*, a small crustacean, undertakes mass migrations against the current, sticking close to the bank and overcoming riffles with the help of turbulence and eddies.

The dimensions of this counter-drift behavior were once illumined, almost literally, by an experiment involving radioactive phosphorous. One week after irradiated bacteria were introduced into a Michigan river, radioactive invertebrates were detected a hundred yards upstream. A week later the radiation had advanced to two hundred yards and was showing up in different organisms. It progressed more quickly through quiet waters than it did through a long riffle. In five weeks' time, contaminated stoneflies and fishflies were detected as far as five hundred yards above the point of introduction—an extended biotic exclamation up one of the gutters of entropy, at what cost to that particular irradiated ecosystem no one knows.

Pacific salmon come from a long lineage. The oldest species known by fossil, *Eosalmo driftwoodensis*, lived fifty million years ago, while Oregon was still tectonically assembling itself. The most dramatic family member to date was *Smilodonicthys rastrosus*, a lunker species that has caused many sport fishermen to investigate time travel. This fish, which swam our waters only five or six million years ago, was ten feet long, weighed five hundred pounds, and was equipped with long fangs—the saber-toothed tiger of salmonids.

Salmon as we know them probably evolved in the course of the last two million years. By one theory, they derive from freshwater fish that took to the sea out of Pleistocene necessity, displaced by glaciers from their native lakes and rivers. Others argue that their anadromous habit is much older, but at some point in evolutionary time, salmonids acquired the capacity to survive in both salt and fresh water and to orient themselves on epic North Pacific travels. It still isn't known how they navigate at sea. Sensitivity to the sun or stars seems unlikely. It may be, some researchers believe, that salmon have somehow attuned themselves to Earth's magnetic field, following pathways of extremely low-voltage current that eventually return each fish to the mouth of its native river system. Close to shore and in fresh water they are probably guided by temperature changes and flow variations, and definitely by an exquisite sense of smell capable of discerning the unique chemical signature of their home waters.

The Pleistocene glaciers left a desolate landscape of gravels and bare basalt. As grasses and shrubs and trees gradually dispersed from unglaciated sanctuaries, salmon pioneered the reopened waterways, adapting to the nuances of individual drainages, fertilizing the gravels with spawn and their own spawned-out bodies. Willows and other riparian vegetation slowly took hold, stabilizing banks and bars. Millennia passed, salmon thronging the rivers in enormous runs that interblended throughout the year. Eventually conifers stood near streams again, their shade moderating water temperatures as the climate warmed, their toppled trunks restraining the erosive power of floods, trapping gravels, forming pools and riffles. Young salmon came of age in the structured streams, gaining strength for their journey by feeding on the carcasses of the old. Raccoons and bears and eagles came for the carcasses, dispersing the rich captured life of the North Pacific deep into woods and mountains. Old-growth forests and mountain meadows are transmutations of the bones and flesh of countless salmon.

A forest or meadow ecosystem, any ecosystem, is a complex abundance tuned toward its own persistence. The system does not immunize its member species and individuals against disaster, but it does weave its lifeways into a many-stranded resilience capable of absorbing disaster and easing its harshest blows. Fire in a healthy forest or prairie is normally not a catastrophe but an agent of renewal, a destroying creator, and floods in a healthy watershed are the same kind of force. They flush sediment downstream and onto the floodplain, where it fertilizes vegetation. They claim new driftwood and rearrange wood already in the river, forming new pools and deepening existing ones, reinvigorating their food webs. And the flood surges of spring carry—or used to carry—numberless juvenile salmon, called smolt, hundreds of miles downstream, the tiny fish relying on the strong currents to get them to their new lives in the Pacific.

The specific means by which floods renew stream ecosystems are still largely unknown. Researchers discover them piecemeal, one at a time, through dedication and good luck. One recent study involved the October caddis, a sizable orange insect relished by adult steelhead. (The steelhead is a large, anadromous form of rainbow trout. A trout is a salmon that stayed in the river. Steelhead are trout who developed a seasonal taste for seafood.) In the spring, caddis larvae graze periphyton as voraciously as sheep graze a pasture. Smaller species of insects get little to eat and fare poorly, and young steelhead, who rely on those small insects—the caddis is too big for them, and too well armored in its case of silk and pebbles—grow only slowly. But if there comes a winter flood of sufficient magnitude to roll sizable rocks in its bedload, those rocks will smash a great many October caddis cases, while doing less damage to the smaller insects, which find refuge in cracks and depressions. In the spring the smaller insects will get a greater portion of periphyton forage, young steelhead will get more to eat and fatten faster, and the steelhead species—along with steelhead fishermen, and other scavengers and predators—will have been well served by the violence of rushing water.

The dams we humans build are intended to restrain that violence, and in that they mainly succeed. But they also mute or eliminate altogether the ecological benefits of floods, and a century and a half of land development has dramatically amplified the damage floods do. The draining and conversion of wetlands for agriculture has forfeited the absorptive value of those natural sponges and laid their soil open to erosion. Building roads along rivers and hardening their channels with levees and dikes merely exports the energy of floods downstream. In the watersheds of the Cascades and Coast Range, clearcuts and logging roads have increased peak stream loads by twenty to thirty percent. A clearcut slope releases ten times the sediment a forested slope will; the hemorrhage declines over time but does not fully heal for thirty years. Logging roads are even more damaging, boosting the chance of landslides by ten- to a hundredfold. Logging road mileage in Oregon national forests has more than tripled since 1960. The total stands at over seventy-three thousand miles.

Erosion in mountain watersheds tends to be punctuated, most of it taking place in concentrated bursts during major deluges. In watersheds riddled with roads and clearcuts, as virtually all of ours are, these epochal storms can cause wildly cascading destruction. Two hours of the benchmark flood of 1964 produced twice as much erosion in western Oregon as would occur in the next thirty *years* combined. The flood of 1996, though lesser than the 1964 event, took a similar toll, and future floods will repeat the tale. Huge river flows are nothing unusual in Oregon. In the flood of 1861, the Willamette River's discharge at Albany was measured at nearly triple the 1996 peak level. A current ran four feet deep through downtown Salem. Every mill in Oregon City was washed away. In 1907 there were three floods in a single year, two of them bigger than 1996. Since 1860 there have been fourteen Oregon floods of the 1996 magnitude or greater, an average of one per decade.

Salmon evolved with floods and by means of floods. Like volcanism and the great ice flows, high water has never daunted them for long, but in this eye blink of evolutionary time we call human, they face grave troubles. A century of logging has suffocated their spawning gravels with silt and raised the crucial water temperatures of formerly shaded streams. A century and a half of ranching and farming has denuded and broken down stream banks, turning cold deep flows into warm shallows, and laced the waters with harmful fertilizers. Riverside industries have exposed salmon to chemical effluents that nothing in their evolutionary past has prepared them for. Dams on the Columbia and Snake, stifling the river currents, kill nine out of ten smolt on their migratory spring journey; dams on those rivers and the Deschutes, Klamath, and Middle Fork Willamette have walled salmon away from major portions of their ancestral habitat. Hatchery fish crowd out the wild populations, spread diseases among them, and dilute their finely tuned genetic heritage through hybridization. Wild salmon still return to their birth waters, but in ragtag remnants of their former runs. The waters no longer support them. The home they made in the Pleistocene is falling apart.

A Brief History of Eden

Many stretches of Oregon's rivers, particularly those listed under the National Wild and Scenic Rivers Act or other protective designations, run free and wild, largely untroubled by human impacts. From the West Little Owyhee in the parched southeastern tablelands to the brief Nestucca in the northern Coast Range, from the Chetco threading through redwoods on the southern coast to the great Snake boiling through Hells Canyon, those rivers look to the hiker or kayaker much as they did when Euro-Americans first came to the Northwest. Only one element is missing. You see few inhabitants in those wild-river places, but a few hundreds or thousands of years ago you would have seen many more. Northwest Indians lived and hunted and fished and foraged in all the watersheds of what we now call Oregon. According to their cultural traditions, their lives in the land went back as far as the lives of the trees and stones. Their bones, like the bones of salmon, have risen into the boughs of pines and Douglas firs and the flowers of wild rhododendrons.

Chinookan and Sahaptian peoples lived along the lower Columbia east through the Gorge, their lives intensely focused on the river. They plied the waters in fifty-foot dugout canoes, speared and netted salmon, and traded with other Northwestern tribes and peoples from as far away as the Great Plains at the major cultural crossroads of Celilo Falls. Eastward, the Tenino made winter villages in the Deschutes and John Day valleys; the Umatilla and Cayuse ranged over the Columbia Plateau; the Nez Perce trapped fish and dug roots in the canyons of the Wallowa and the Minam, Joseph Creek and the Grande Ronde. Shoshones and Bannocks took salmon from the Snake River, trout and insects from the streams of the Blue Mountains. Nomadic bands of Northern Paiutes wandered Oregon's hardest country, its southeast quarter, gathering cattails, rice grass, and wild cabbage from moist oases by streams and lakes, holing up in winter rock shelters in the Owyhee canyons. Klamaths and Modocs lived in the milder south-central region, harvesting pods of *wokas*, the yellow water lily, on Klamath Lake, fishing and lodging on the Sprague, the Williamson, and the quiet Lost River that can't decide where it wants to go.

West of the Cascades, the Takelma inhabited the Rogue and Applegate and Illinois drainages; their name means "those who dwell along the river." The Umpqua took their living from the two-forked river of that name, running the currents in maneuverable canoes. The Molalla, recent fugitives from the east, were centered in the McKenzie and Santiam and Clackamas watersheds of the western Cascade slope. The great wetland that was the Willamette Valley was home to the nine bands of the Kalapuya, who gathered the edible bulbs of camas and other staples and regularly burned the lush prairies to keep them vigorous. (Kalapuya means "long grasses.") And along the coast, several peoples — from south to north, the Tututni, Coos, Siuslaw, Alsea, Tillamook, and Clatsop — lived on salmon, seals, and other bounty of the tidal rivers that flowed into what some of them knew as the great river with one bank.

All these native cultures depended on rivers, and everything that lured Euro-American outsiders to the Oregon Country also had to do with rivers. The first seekers were sea captains looking for the Strait of Anian, the legendary Northwest Passage obsessively imagined for centuries by European monarchs and explorers. They came and went, leaving diseases, a few shipwrecks, and a scattering of their genes. The first seafarer to enter the Columbia, the American Robert Gray, came in quest of sea otter pelts for the China trade. (The otter then ranged upriver to Celilo Falls.) Lewis and Clark arrived with their Corps of Discovery via the Snake and Columbia, finding salmon "jumping very thick." Though they failed Thomas Jefferson's charge to find "the direct water communication from sea to sea formed by the bed of the Missouri, and perhaps the Oregon," they did discover, in Lewis's phrase, "the most practicable Route such as Nature has permitted." And they put the Oregon Country, and some of its Columbia Basin rivers, literally on the map.

From 1811, when John Jacob Astor's men established a trading post at Astoria, through the 1830s, trappers and traders found their way into almost every river drainage in Oregon in search of beaver. The Willamette Valley was trapped out quickly. Alexander McLeod, exploring drainages to the south in 1826, was thwarted only by the Siuslaw, which was too choked with fallen trees to penetrate. He was seeking a rumored great southern river that might be navigable for trade — a diminished version of the Northwest Passage. He found the Rogue and was badly disappointed. Peter Skene Ogden also searched for "the big river," which he called the Clammite; he eventually found the headwaters of the Klamath, but no navigable stream. Ogden and others thoroughly explored east of the Cascades, opening trade routes from the Columbia south to Klamath Lake and up the John Day valley into the Malheur drainage. The most significant track pioneered by the trappers led from the Snake River up the Burnt River and Alder Creek to the Powder and the Grande Ronde Valley, then over the Blues to the Umatilla and the Columbia. This route would soon become part of the Oregon Trail.

Methodist missionaries arrived in the 1830s and looked along rivers for what they desired: tillable soil and souls in need of conversion. At French Prairie and the falls of the Willamette they found good soil but few souls, the Kalapuya having been rendered virtually extinct by Euro-American diseases. That meant little Indian resistance, and a confirmed sense of Manifest Destiny, for the waves of settlers that pulsed annually into the Willamette Valley during the 1840s. For the settlers, the stiffest natural resistance came, cruelly enough, at the end of the six-month trek, when the weakened immigrants were on the verge of success. Before the Barlow Road opened in 1846, many had to take to the Columbia River at the Dalles on rafts or in makeshift boats. The Columbia was a wild river then. Many families lost everything they owned at the Cascades, a fierce three-mile rapid now drowned behind Bonneville Dam. A good many lost their lives.

Those who made it spread southward through the New Eden of the Willamette Valley, running livestock in prairie grasses that reached above the animals' backs, building log homes not near the river but along the valley's forested, foothilled margins. Many settlers had been flooded out of the Mississippi Valley and weren't about to repeat their mistake. The broad and braided Willamette rose out of its banks regularly, leaving water standing for months in sloughs and oxbows. Later arrivals, forced to claim in the floodplain, set to work digging drainage ditches and gradually brought the moist earth under the plow. As their livelihoods progressed, other lives declined. One settler wrote at mid-century that the valley had "largely ceased to be the home of the crane, curlew, gray plover, and even the snipe, as well as the beaver, muskrat, and wild duck."

Gold was discovered in the Rogue River country in 1851, drawing flurries of prospectors to tributary junctions throughout the watershed; the slaughter or deportation of almost all Indians in the region followed in short order. In the 1860s richer pay streaks showed themselves in northeastern Oregon, in Baker County and on the John Day River. Some operations, placer and hard rock, produced millions of dollars in yellow metal over the course of several decades. Ditches up to a hundred miles long were dug to convey water for hydraulic mining, which ate away the sides of stream valleys, and riverbeds were turned upside down by dredging operations. The streams of this part of the state were lucky that their gold was not more plentiful. To see why, visit the Powder River and its tributary, Cracker Creek, near the town of Sumpter. You'll find their channels heaped high with dumps of gravel, cobbles, and boulders in continuous mounds that look for all the world like castings from a gigantic earthworm.

Another kind of mining boom exploded on the Columbia and other coastal rivers in the 1860s. Canning technology arrived from California, and with it came industrial salmon fishing. The rivers were rigged and plied with gill nets, pound nets, and horse-drawn purse seines; on the Columbia, perpetual-motion fish wheels, powered by the river's current, scooped out ton after flopping ton of salmon. The young state's export of canned salmon soared to nearly half a million cases a year by the 1870s, almost twenty-four million pounds of fish. The runs remained huge and continuous compared to those today, but nonetheless in 1875 the modern era of fishery management was born. The Oregon legislature asked the U. S. Fish Commission to investigate the diminishing Columbia River salmon runs. The commission recommended building a hatchery, and hatcheries would become the problematic axiom of twentieth-century salmon-fishery policy.

Steamships came to the Columbia, Willamette, and larger coastal rivers in the 1850s, and the U. S. Army Corps of Engineers was recruited to dredge channels and remove all the snags and drift trees they could. By the 1860s people and freight could travel by steamer up the Willamette to Corvallis (to Eugene at high water), and, with mule or rail portages at the Cascades and Celilo Falls, up the Columbia and lower Snake clear to Lewiston, Idaho.

River transport and the railroads that followed encouraged a bounceback migration into Eastern Oregon, the Willamette Valley being claimed out. Slow at first, the influx quickened once the unaccountably disagreeable Modocs, Nez Perce, Bannocks, and Shoshones had been subdued in the 1870s. Hopeful ranchers settled by every stream and spring; in twenty years their sheep and cattle had grazed out much of the bunch grass, laying the ecosystem open to the sagebrush and cheat grass that dominate it today. Public lands grazing continued unregulated until 1934 and remains under-regulated now, doing severe injury to rangelands and streams. Dry country takes a long time to heal. Irrigation for pasture and crop farming became a traditional way of life east of the mountains, buttressed by first-in-time water rights. Diversion dams and pumps now deplete some rivers and streams to midsummer trickles. Groundwater is also tapped, lowering the water table and sending runoff loaded with silt, pesticides, and fertilizers into the rivers.

Oregon's timber industry started, slowly, toward the end of the 1800s. Big riverside old growth was first to fall, Sitka spruce and red cedar and Douglas fir, the mammoth logs rafted downstream to the mills. As cutting proceeded up the Coast Range and Cascade slopes, splash dams came into use: a small stream was dammed into a big pond where logs were dumped, then the dam was breached and a torrent of logs shot down to the river, leaving a reamed-out channel of mud and bedrock. World War I brought the first big boom, driving up the price of timberland by a factor of ten. Big corporations bought major holdings and logged them off with little reforestation, punching roads and muddying streams in many watersheds. More than half of Oregon's jobs were wood products jobs. The housing boom after World War II gave the industry another boost and, private holdings having been thoroughly mined, spread clearcuts into previously roadless areas of the national forests and other public lands, which make up fifty percent of the state of Oregon. Steeper slopes were sheared, shallower soils exposed, and road after road carelessly built, the bladed earth dumped down the mountainsides. Timber was king in Oregon for a hundred years. The economy prospered, for the most part, but streams and watersheds are paying the price of that prosperity and will be for decades to come.

And they are paying in other ways. Our century has dammed the Oregon-border portion of the Columbia in four places, turning that stretch of America's second-greatest river into a string of slackwater lakes. Our electrical power is relatively cheap; young salmon, in a caricature of nature, are collected and barged around the dams. Pulp mills and food processing plants contribute jobs and essential products; their effluents contribute poisonous chemicals and smothering nutrient loads. Roads and highways take us anywhere we want to go, following rivers and diking them off from their floodplains, forcing them to incise their channels. In the cities our toilets flush cleanly; during storm flows they flush directly into rivers. New malls, new roads, new suburban expansions make a good life available to many; they also make the land unavailable to absorb water as it once did, thus contributing hydrocarbons and other pollutants in runoff that reaches streams quickly and augments destructive flooding.

If everything we have done to our rivers in the course of two hundred years had occurred overnight, we would be horrified, stricken with grief. But the changes have come gradually, incrementally, hardly perceptible from year to year, from decade to decade. As the changes occur, we adjust. We take as normal the rivers that now flow through our lives, hardly aware that the river any child grows up with is likely to be muddier, more engineered, more polluted, and less rich in life than the river his father or grandmother knew. The rivers we tax the hardest for our needs and conveniences have been slowly slipping away for a long time, and as they have slipped we have lost the reference point that our predecessors didn't think necessary: What does a healthy river look like? And so the healthiest rivers remaining, those that our history has touched least, are not merely images of beauty. They are the best available standards of Oregon's natural integrity, benchmarks of its past that could guide us as we try to imagine and give birth to its future.

A Place in the Rivered Land

The protection of rivers was a late-blooming priority in the course of the twentieth-century conservation movement, despite the fact that several of the movement's formative battles were sparked by dam-building projects. In 1913 the damming of the Tuolumne River in the California Sierra Nevada, and the consequent inundation of Yosemite's Hetch Hetchy Valley, aroused cries of outrage from John Muir and his young Sierra Club. Forty years later, a proposal for two dams in Dinosaur National Monument forged conservationists into a broad activist coalition, spurred the publication of Sierra Club books, and brought the modern movement of age. The issue in each case, though, was less the river itself than the sanctity of the national park through which it flowed. Conservationists were focused on setting aside parcels of land as parks and wilderness, and most of those parcels were in high-elevation mountainous terrain with streams but few long stretches of river. Rivers flowed through the hard-worked valleys where we lived; parks and wilderness were somewhere else, where we went to get away.

By midcentury, though, American rivers had been so thoroughly dredged, channelized, filled, polluted, dammed, and diverted that a movement arose to protect the freest and purest stretches that remained. The original intent, modeled on the idea of wilderness designation, was to set aside the crown jewels — the singular, spectacular wild rivers of our part of the North American continent. That idea was expanded in the 1960s to include reaches of river that had seen some development but were still free-flowing and hadn't entirely lost their wild character. The National Wild and Scenic Rivers Act passed Congress in 1968 with the enthusiastic assent of President Lyndon Johnson, designating sections of twelve rivers as charter members of the National Wild and Scenic Rivers System and identifying others for study. Among the original twelve was an eighty-four-mile section of the lower Rogue River, preserving its dramatic passage through Oregon's Klamath Mountains to the Pacific.

The Wild and Scenic Rivers Act recognizes three classes of protected status: wild rivers, defined as "vestiges of primitive America"; scenic rivers, less wild but largely undeveloped; and recreational rivers, readily accessible and generally more altered by human activity. Designated rivers are shielded from dams, hydroelectric diversions, channelization, and other harmful impacts on the river itself. As for land uses along the river, the managing public agencies — as many as fifteen may be involved for a single river — generally grandfather in existing uses but limit or prohibit new or expanded uses. A protective corridor extends one-quarter mile to each side of the river, or rim to rim of the river's canyon if it has one. On federal lands, no logging can occur within the corridor of a wild river; scenic and recreational classifications permit limited logging. Restrictions on mining are similar —claims existing prior to designation are not extinguished. Recreational access may be limited at an agency's discretion to prevent overuse of the river and its corridor. Private water rights are unaffected, except that the government secures to itself the right to maintain in-stream flow.

From the original twelve in 1968, the Wild and Scenic Rivers System has grown to include more than three hundred and thirty stretches of rivers and tributaries. Oregon's share of these is out of proportion to its size: about sixty designated rivers and tributaries, the most in any state including Alaska. (Counts vary among agencies and conservationists because the components of a watershed can be broken down, on a map, in different ways.)

The Oregon system grew slowly at first. In 1975, with the creation of Hells Canyon National Recreation Area, the Hells Canyon portion of the Snake joined the Rogue as our second listed river (and thereby escaped a dam already authorized for the lower canyon). Reaches of the Illinois and Owyhee were designated as part of wilderness legislation in 1984. And then the deluge. Jimmy Carter, late in his presidency, called for an expanded wild and scenic system, spurring the Forest Service and other federal agencies to evaluate thousands of rivers for possible inclusion. The Oregon Rivers Council (now the Pacific Rivers Council) used Forest Service studies to persuade Senator Mark Hatfield to sponsor the Oregon Omnibus Rivers Act of 1988, which in one fell swoop added stretches of forty-four rivers plus nine tributaries to the national system, the most ever brought under protection at one time outside the state of Alaska.

That same year, conservationist Bill Marlett and the Oregon Natural Resources Council (now Oregon Wild) launched a successful ballot initiative that expanded the Oregon Scenic Waterways System, which provides overlapping safeguards at the state level for several federally listed rivers, and constitutes the only protection for a handful of others, including the Nestucca on the north coast. It was an altogether phenomenal year for the flowing waters of our state, an environmental achievement that ranks alongside the landmark first-in-the-nation bottle-return bill and land-use planning legislation of the 1970s. Oregon's breakthrough placed it in the forefront of river conservation nationally and inspired similar omnibus efforts in several other states.

And yet, two decades after that breakthrough, the Oregon wild and scenic system is nothing very vast. Of thirty-five thousand miles of streams and rivers big enough to bear names, only eighteen hundred and fifty miles, or five percent, are included in the system. That far exceeds the national figure of six-tenths of one percent, but it's a large number only by comparison. Why, after the most successful river conservation campaign in history, and the heightened public awareness that came with it, do ninety-five percent of our river miles remain unprotected?

The answers have to do with landownership and its extractive uses. On federal lands, where most eligible rivers flow, wild and scenic designation raises a limited but real impediment to logging, mining, and grazing.

Resource industries historically have had easy access to raw materials on these lands, due to a tilted doctrine of multiple use. That tilt has to some extent been righted in the last twenty years, but institutional inertia and industry lobbying still exert a powerful counterforce against change. The Forest Service has identified a hundred Oregon river sections, beyond those already designated, eligible for wild and scenic consideration. Only a handful have been designated since 1988. The process grinds slowly through year after year of studies, hearings, and stalemate.

Private property ownership is another sticking point. The Wild and Scenic Rivers Act was intended to put a cap on development, not to eliminate development already in place, and the government's favored tool toward that end is the purchase of easements that disallow new or intensified construction on private holdings along designated rivers. The act also, however, authorizes outright land acquisition through eminent domain. That power has been used sparingly, mostly in the first few years of the act's existence, and usually to block large-scale development presenting a major threat to a river's natural character. But the knowledge that eminent domain can be and has been asserted makes property owners understandably skittish about the prospect of wild and scenic designation. They might be more receptive if the government were to renounce eminent domain and work with easements only, emphasizing to landowners that a river whose natural integrity has been secured against unwanted encroachments of commerce will enhance, not diminish, the value of their holdings.

But Oregon's wild and scenic river system will continue to grow, if slowly. Far more troubling than the limited extent of the system is its limited effectiveness as a shield against ecological injury. Designation has blocked dams and other engineering projects on several Oregon rivers, but it has been much less successful in preventing less dramatic, more gradual degradation. Logging and mining and overgrazing occur, legally and illegally, within the protected half-mile corridors of some of our listed rivers, and they occur close outside the corridors of almost all of them. Aerial photos of the lower Rogue show a growing patchwork of clearcuts and logging roads on both sides of the narrow, sinuous swath of the river's canyon. Stripping steep mountainsides within a river's watershed is to damage the river itself. Human beings may or may not respect a line on a map. Sediment, debris torrents, and water too warm for fish definitely do not.

Only a scant few of our listed streams are designated from source to mouth, and a majority of those are short tributaries. Most of the rivers are protected only in a section or two, usually along their upper reaches on public lands; their middle and lower reaches, where most of us live, receive the accumulating uses and abuses of our economic activity. It is a very good thing that forty miles of the upper Rogue have been protected since 1988. It is a very good thing that eighty-four miles of the lower Rogue have been protected since 1968. But only a third of those miles are managed as wild river, and the undesignated remainder of the river, its ninety-mile midsection, is not protected at all. The Rogue's water quality was declining before its listing and has continued to decline since. Its salmon and steelhead runs, with sporadic annual exceptions, have dropped more sharply since designation than they were dropping before. The Rogue is still a great river, one of the most beautiful in the world, but no ecologist would call it a healthy river.

Health is a relative condition, of course. The Rogue River is in better shape than many. Its listing as wild and scenic has very possibly slowed its ecological decline, and that is a meaningful accomplishment. It should be sobering, though, that the most sanguine judgment that can be made about a forty-year charter member of the National Wild and Scenic Rivers System is that it may be deteriorating at a reduced pace.

We engage a river at particular places — bends, holes, rapids, bars, falls. The nouns get vaguer when we try to identify longer parts — reaches, stretches — and become geometrically abstract when we divide a river according to political and economic concerns: sections, segments. Rivers will not hold still for sectioning or segmentation. They are creatures of length, of continuity. To address the health of rivers we must address them in their wholeness, and that means we must deal with ourselves. All of us live in watersheds.

Stream ecologists are working out an idea they call the river continuum concept, which suggests that all rivers, or most at least, share a common ecological gradient along their lengths. From the rills and streamlets of origin to the broad river near its mouth, there is evidence that predictable changes in life communities occur. Shaded headwaters regions, structured by stones and fallen wood, host a guild of invertebrates known as shredders, who begin to break down the crucial leaf- and needle-fall that fuels the stream's organic economy. Small particles of that matter are filtered from the current far downstream, in the river's middle reaches, by a guild of collectors. The wider channel receives more sunlight in these reaches, producing more organic matter from within. Periphyton grows more abundantly, supporting a guild of grazers, and various plants take root in sediments the milder-sloped river deposits. Lower still, where the accomplished river travels its floodplain, its ecology grades into further changes only poorly understood, that zone of the continuum having been less studied and usually more disturbed by human activity.

The science of stream ecology is still young, and the river continuum concept is one of its newest hypotheses. It needs testing, refinement, elaboration, but its essential premise makes sense: Rivers have something like a common genotype, a graded biological form associated with their graded fluvial form from source to mouth. The lives and systems of lives you find at a particular river place are not arbitrary; they are flourishing where they belong in the organism that is the river.

And where do we humans belong? How do we belong, and how should we belong? It is not arbitrary that we live as closely associated with rivers as we do. As far back as ancient Egypt and Babylonia, and farther still, our cultures have been built on the floodplains of rivers, on the ruins of continents slowly on their way to the sea. In the modern world our relationship with rivers extends from the high dendritic branchings of their drainages down along each meander and valley to the rich mixed waters of their estuaries. For better or worse, we are members of the river continuum. So far, it has been better for us, worse for the rivers and their other members. For that there is plenty of blame to go around. All of us have taken rivers for granted. All of us have participated in their exploitation. The light I'm writing by, the paper I'm writing on, the studs and rafters in the house around me, the food on my table — these and much more have come to me at some cost to rivers, including, no doubt, rivers I regularly notice and admire without thinking about how my way of life might burden them.

None of us, though, not one of us, ever set out deliberately to harm a river, and neither did those who came before. We set out only to live our lives and make our livings, and, despite all we have done to them, we love our rivers. In the Northwest we are never far from the lilt and swirl of living water. Whether to fish or swim or paddle, or only to stand and gaze, to glance as we cross a bridge, all of us are drawn to rivers, all of us happily submit to their spell. We need their familiar mystery. We need their fluent lives intermingling with our own.

The National Wild and Scenic Rivers System, and other protective mantles, are expressions of our love. They constitute a first, halting recognition of the vulnerability of rivers and our thoughtless excesses that do them harm. In those unwieldy categories of law — wild, scenic, recreational — we are groping toward right relationship, a way of being that acknowledges our legitimate uses and sets careful limits on them. We are groping toward responsible membership in the river continuum, and we must find our way further. We have learned to cherish wild rivers; those fountains of natural joy must always run free. We fail those rivers, though, if we continue to fail their lower reaches, the valleys where we work and live, the rivers of home. The river above and the river below are nothing different. The river is always one, and we fail it if we fail to rejoin its segments, to expand its corridor, to appreciate the entirety of its length and breadth and complexity. We will save our rivers only if we follow flowing water's mysterious way of fingering into land and learn the nature of its belonging, so that the continuum might flow on with us as part of it.

THE SPIRIT OF RIVERS

Anything of Nature reflects the viewer, but of all the natural lives,
rivers return the surest image of the human.
They are spirits in motion, bound up like ours in the labor
of time, steadily being born and steadily dying.
Like us at our best, they are true to themselves
under all conditions, changeful and changeless,
constrained and free, a lively resurgent presence
of past and future made one. To seek a river's source
is to seek our own, to turn and turn and always return—
to snow and mountains, to sea and sky, and always to water,
to the soul's deep springs, always to the flowing
ungraspable image that forever runs free of all names
and knowing, singing the story of its own being,
bearing forth from distant passages its mortal and infinite nature.

III

Writing Life

The Prankster-in-Chief Moves On

The answer is never the answer. I've never seen anybody really find the answer — they think they have, so they stop thinking. But the job is to seek mystery, evoke mystery, plant a garden in which strange plants grow and mysteries bloom. The need for mystery is greater than the need for an answer.

Ken Kesey

Ken Kesey was dressed in white from head to toe when I first met him, in the spring of 1979, at the first and only Southern Oregon Writers Conference in Klamath Falls, which a friend and I had organized. A broad tank of a man with a fringe of sandy curls around his balding head, carrying some extra weight but otherwise looking every bit the collegiate wrestler he once had been, Kesey talked at dinner about farming and especially about sheep, the purity of their innocence, how we needed that in our lives. There was a Christian flavor to his remarks. He likened himself to a retired country squire. I, tuned to his every word with the hunger of an unpublished novice, was disappointed. This was my psychedelic hero, the progenitor of McMurphy and Stamper, the Prankster-in-Chief on the legendary bus called Furthur?

But in the fiction workshop he said some things I've never forgotten. He asked what we were reading. "You!" somebody hollered. Well, Kesey replied, why are you reading me? If you want to write you should be reading Melville and Hawthorne, Shakespeare, the King James Bible. You should go to the source. Listen, he said, his enthusiasm gathering, when you sit down to write you're inside a bubble, see? And the bubble lives outside of time, outside the little room where you're writing, and with you in that bubble are the greatest, the truly original writers—if you've read them. That, he told us, is the possibility, the pure potential of creative writing. We knew he had been there. He lifted us, and challenged us, with that directive.

On the second day of the conference, perhaps a bit worn down by short stories such as mine, which was about a man who kills a woman and forgets it and climbs a mountain and remembers and freezes to death, Kesey said, "People, listen. It comes down to this. If it doesn't uplift the human heart, *piss* on it."

He was then forty-four. It had been twelve years since he had resettled on the farm near Pleasant Hill where he had grown up in the 1940s and '50s, doing magic acts onstage—a showman from the start—at the McDonald Theater in Eugene, and later wrestling for the University of Oregon and almost making the 1960 U. S. Olympic team. In 1958, twenty-three years old, Kesey moved to California with his wife, Faye Haxby, with whom he had eloped two years before. He brought an unpublished novel and a lot of ambition and attitude to Wallace Stegner's graduate creative writing program at Stanford University, and a couple of years later he enrolled in a different curriculum—Army- or CIA-sponsored tests at a Veterans Administration hospital on the effects of psychoactive drugs, for which he received seventy-five dollars a session.

The Defense Department wanted to know if LSD could be useful in espionage and prisoner interrogations. It's unknown if Kesey helped them to an answer, but it's certain that he became an instant advocate of exploring the inner wilderness of the psyche, and fundamentally changing society, by means of LSD. When he hired on as a night aide in the psychiatric ward of the hospital, he recognized the kinship between psychedelic awareness and psychosis: The patients were lost explorers. Kesey began a story about life in such a ward, a story that wouldn't cohere until one night, in a peyote-induced vision, he conjured a schizophrenic American Indian he called Chief Bromden. He had a narrator and he had a novel.

The miracle of *One Flew Over the Cuckoo's Nest* is, first, that a guy could write a novel while regularly blasting his head with hallucinogens; and, second, that he could write a very fine novel in which psychedelic consciousness, deftly and aptly incorporated, is essential to the tale. He captures its paranoiac aura in the subtle click and hum of machinery Chief Bromden hears in the asylum walls, and in the "microscopic wires and grids and transistors . . . designed to dissolve on contact with air" the chief imagines when he crushes one of the daily sedatives Big Nurse force-feeds her inmates. And he evokes just as tellingly the expansive, synesthetic happiness of the psychedelic high, as when Randle Patrick McMurphy first enters the joint and bellows his vast laugh — "free and loud and it comes out of his wide grinning mouth and spreads in rings bigger and bigger till it's lapping against the walls all over the ward."

Kesey had the mental and emotional strength to harness for his art the experience that reduced most of us to wordlessness — an indication, surely, of a sense of self and purpose as powerful as his physical being, and this in a writer in his mid-twenties. But the book came to full fruition, it turns out, in the ordinary way — through hard work. According to Malcolm Cowley, the Stanford professor Kesey liked best, he wrote long patches of the novel "at top speed," often under the influence, but returned to those drafts later to add, delete, correct, and rewrite, responding to Cowley's observations and his own, un-spaced-out judgment. The canard that Kesey never revised his first drafts, in the fashion of some of the Beats, has flourished far too long.

Cuckoo's Nest, tapping perfectly the temper of the times with its cosmology of a tight-assed freedom-hating Combine running the country, was published in 1962 to enormous acclaim and sales. Hard on its heels two years later came a second novel, *Sometimes a Great Notion*. Kesey had returned to Oregon, lived in logging camps, and re-frequented the haunts of his youth to write it. *Cuckoo's Nest* is perhaps the better-achieved book, but *Notion*, for me, is the greater achievement—a sprawling, boisterous, multigenerational story of a Coast Range logging family pitted against its community, of one brother locking horns with another, and of East Coast culture at odds with earthy, implacable, Western stubbornness. These tensions play out in a place—landscape, weather, biota—as intimately and animatedly evoked as any in literature. If *Cuckoo's Nest* shines with the moral clarity of parable, *Notion* has the variegated texture, heroic proportions, and moral complexity of epic myth. The book's ambition is evident in the method of its telling, which has time sliding freely backward and forward and point of view slipping continually among several characters, including a dog and an eerie, Whitmanesque omniscient observer who sees everything, right down to blackberry roots deepening their hold in the rain-sodden earth.

Sometimes a Great Notion trips now and then on its special effects. It is overlong and in parts overwritten. But it fairly vibrates with the life and land of the Pacific Northwest, and it is, like *One Flew Over the Cuckoo's Nest*, one of the best novels I know.

"I don't think I'll ever be able to do that again," Kesey told an interviewer, and he wasn't. Two books in two years seemed to exhaust his artistry—or maybe just redirected it. As the first (very mixed) reviews of *Notion* appeared in 1964, Kesey and his band of co-spirited Merry Pranksters were cavorting cross-country in a 1939 International Harvester school bus lushly painted with dazzling day-glo colors, dropping acid, taking footage for a movie, and demonstrating to the heartland their version of the new consciousness, a journey well-chronicled by Tom Wolfe in *The Electric Kool-Aid Acid Test*. The bus was named Furthur; a sign on the back read CAUTION: WEIRD LOAD. Back in California later that year, Kesey and the Pranksters spread the news through a series of Acid Tests, serving up LSD—until October 1966 still perfectly legal—in smoking punchbowls of Kool-Aid on dry ice, as strobe lights flickered and phantasmagoric images pulsed liquidly on the dancehall walls to the music of a new band first called the Warlocks and later the Grateful Dead. The aesthetics of the psychedelic era, as well as wider use of the drugs, derived in large part from the Furthur expedition and the Acid Tests.

For many of us who were introduced to LSD and its ilk in the '60s, or who introduced ourselves, the psychedelic experience was a mixed and at times harrowing thing. My dorm-mates and I at Reed College burdened our explorations with an interpretive framework involving the *Tibetan Book of the Dead*, which was to guide us through the *bardos* of ego death to the clear white light and back again. It never worked for me. More than once I was reduced for a time — a timeless time — to a quivering puddle of fear, quite certain that I was forever lost from my life. Psychedelics awakened me to spiritual awareness, an immense gift, but they also fragmented my accustomed and still-forming sense of being, leaving me with a vision of happiness — a human community of love and trust, beyond fear — but pretty distant from happiness itself. Kesey and his cohorts, it seemed from afar, were living that vision. They got the *dance* of the experience, its truest lesson, and showed the way like joyous pioneers, standing up to the forces of cultural reaction seemingly without fear. In doing so they showed the rare courage — few others had it, Allen Ginsberg being one — to risk being ridiculed and taken for fools.

But the forces of cultural reaction had muscle to flex, and they came at Kesey hard. When two pot-possession raps early in 1966 brought him face to face with a possible five-year prison term, he faked his suicide and fled to safety across the Mexican border. He stayed eight months, joined by his family and a handful of friends, before smuggling himself north again, on horseback, in the persona of a drunken cowboy with a guitar strapped across his back. Making unscheduled public appearances in the Bay Area, evading the law for a while, the avatar of Better Living Through Chemistry threw one last Acid Test. But in this one, a sedate affair on Halloween night 1966, Kesey for the first time preached limits. He billed it as a graduation event, meant to convey to the faithful and the curious that the time had come to move beyond the frequent use of psychedelics.

Collared by authorities, Kesey answered for his pot busts by serving a negotiated six months in the San Mateo County Jail and sheriff's work detail. When he'd done his time, his enthusiasms perhaps just slightly dampened, he came home to Oregon and his father's farm, where he settled in with Faye to raise their children.

In the '70s he wrote magazine pieces, mainly, many of them elegiac about what the counterculture had been and rueful about what it was becoming—random destructiveness, hard drug use, many of the famous and the nameless dying of overdoses. In a story called "The Day After Superman Died"—the reference is to Neal Cassady, the legendary "Fastestmanalive," hero of Jack Kerouac's *On the Road* and driver of Furthur on the Pranksters' 1964 trek—Kesey has a tense standoff with two hippies who drop by the farm on their way home from the Woodstock music festival, a young airhead and an older, tattooed, rotten-toothed Mansonlike jerk. The atmosphere is all irony and apocalypse—a pall of acrid smoke from burning grass fields, Kesey unable to find his "colored glasses," a lamb inexplicably dead, the Beach Boys singing "Good Vibrations" on a tinny radio, and then a friend arrives with news that the great Cassady, doped-up in Mexico, has died of exposure on a pathetic expedition to count railroad ties.

In the story, Kesey's conservative friend from Stanford days, the novelist Larry McMurtry, asks in a letter, "What has the Good Old Revolution been doing lately?"

"Losing," is all Kesey can think to reply.

Or changing form, moving on to the next stage. Kesey had cranked up his tractor, acquired a small fleet of long, low convertibles—he preferred Cadillacs—for getting around his farm, and applied himself to the raising of cattle and sheep and the growing of blueberries. As his kids went through the Pleasant Hill schools he served on school board committees. He helped coach wrestling—not officially or by invitation—and cheered for both sides at football games. He spoke, whenever asked, at high school commencement ceremonies. He used his stature in various ways to help local businesses. For more than three decades he and Faye lived a life of engagement with family and community and the land, a life that offers very lean pickings to those '6os-vilifiers who would tag him as an irresponsible misleader of otherwise virtuous American youngsters.

Ken Kesey showed himself to be, in the best and most basic sense of the term, a conservative. He did not renounce psychedelic drugs. (Later in life, it's said, he liked a dose just potent enough to tremble the leaves at their edges.) He did not renounce his distrust of power and authority, or his flair for outrageous antics. He most certainly did not renounce the essential '6os vision that valued community over corporate profits, peace and tolerance over war and fearfulness, a sense of life's beauty and mystery over the customary trappings of career, money, and piles of possessions. He tried to conserve what he thought best in the cultural upheaval he had so boldly assisted and melded that into the culture he had grown up in and to which he had returned. He planted his values in place and community, even as Furthur, the original bus, sank slowly into a swale on his farm, young trees growing up around it.

Kesey even taught for a year at the University of Oregon, violating his own youthful analysis of what he had learned at Stanford from Wallace Stegner: "Just never to teach in college." He and Stegner had clashed from the beginning—inevitably, given their differences, the one a brash drug-taking rebel buzzing with Beat energy, the other a dignified elder of conservative temperament (though politically liberal) who had taught at Harvard and founded the creative writing program at Stanford. Stegner saw Kesey as talented but undisciplined, a wastrel. "I was never sympathetic to any of his ideas," Stegner recalled years later, "because I thought many of his ideas were half-baked." Kesey saw Stegner as the epitome of academic staidness and convention. "When we headed off on a bus to deal with the future of our synapses," Kesey remarked in 1993, "we knew that Wally wasn't liking what we were doing and that was good enough for us."

Stanford University, as the 1950s turned into the '6os, had the strongest concentration of fiction-writing talent in its history: Robert Stone,

Ernest Gaines, Larry McMurtry, Tillie Olsen, Ed McClanahan, and Wendell Berry, along with Kesey and others, shared the oval seminar table with Wallace Stegner at various times during that era. Most of them appreciated both men. "Stegner saw Kesey as a threat to civilization and intellectualism and sobriety," Robert Stone told Stegner's first biographer, Jackson Benson. "And Ken was a threat to all those values. But what was going on around Ken was so exciting that we were not about to line up against each other on ideological grounds."

Both Kesey and Stegner in later years wrote or said that too much had been made of the fractiousness between them. "We got along in class perfectly well," Stegner told Jackson Benson. "I liked his writing most of the time very well." And Kesey, when I asked him once if Stegner had been a good teacher, replied, "He was better than a teacher. He was like Vince Lombardi, and we were the Green Bay Packers of fiction writing." Kesey gave that same answer, publicly, many times. On another occasion, though, when I asked on the phone why it was they hadn't gotten along, Kesey replied: "Because I was a better writer than him."

The trouble between the two, I think now, may have stemmed as much from their likeness as it did from their differences. Each had made his way to Stanford from inauspicious beginnings in the rural West, Kesey from Colorado and Oregon, Stegner from Saskatchewan and Utah and spells in other places. Both were relatively unproven—Kesey a charismatic and gifted wannabe, Stegner with a notable career in progress but years short of winning his Pulitzer Prize and National Book Award and a place in the American canon. And each had arrived at Stanford's citadel of learning with an attitude stamped into his soul. Stegner's was: When you begin with nothing you'd better value your chances and work, work, work. Kesey's was: Watch out, stay yourself, or power and high culture will suck out your life.

There's validity in both.

I began my '60s as a wannabe Keseyan, all about personal freedom, antiestablishmentism, and self-discovery. I believed in revelation, through

LSD (I took my first trip in October 1966, just as the stuff was illegalized) and through love, but I knew the transient feeling of love much better than I knew the practice of love. I ended my '60s—in the 1970s, like most of us who came of age in that time—by slowly and belatedly embracing the discipline of creative writing and a long-term commitment to another human being and to a particular place or two on Earth. I still took drugs, still reveled in personal autonomy, but I tempered the unbounded pursuit of the future of my synapses with a developing appreciation of what human synapses and spirit had accomplished through past centuries in a gathering field of tradition, and I began to define myself, and challenge myself, thereby. I took a turn in Stegner's direction, as had Kesey—though he wouldn't have seen it that way—after he resettled in Oregon in the late '60s.

I doubt that Stegner and Kesey, brought together at a neutral site in the 1980s, could have suddenly appreciated each other. The gap in temperament and style was too severe. They had both sent too much static into the air, their egos too aroused. Now, with both men gone, it hardly matters. I knew Stegner better, but I'm with Robert Stone. I feel no contradiction in declaring my allegiance to both.

Many who knew them share that assessment. The Green Bay Packers of fiction writing stayed variously bonded over the decades, and when Wendell Berry came to give a reading in Eugene in the fall of 2000 with his wife, Tanya, Marilyn and I attended the dinner in Berry's honor. Ken and Faye Kesey were there; to see them had been part of the motivation for Berry, who doesn't travel a lot doing readings. Kesey, in the best restaurant in Eugene, was dressed in what for him was traditional clothing, a style he'd been wearing since the '60s—a vest made of the material of an American flag, spread tight by his portly figure, and a leather cap. Slowed by a recent stroke, he was not garrulous, more warm than brash. He spoke of improving his vision by stretching the corners of his eyes to the side and pressing on his eyelids in certain ways with his fingers. In this way, he said, he could read without glasses. (This works, I have found, but is impractical for reading sessions of any length and does attract attention in restaurants.)

The day after the dinner, Marilyn and I tagged along with the Berrys to visit the Keseys at their farm. We stopped first at the inconspicuous strip mall in Pleasant Hill where Kesey's company, Intrepid Trips, was headquartered. Kesey and Prankster associates were processing e-mailed orders for a new video from the epic 1964 journey in Furthur—Neal Cassady rapping, a visit with Timothy Leary in New York State, party scenes with Jack Kerouac and Allen Ginsberg. The footage we saw—chaotic, herky-jerky, imperfectly focused—suggested that the LSD experience might better have been served by filmmakers not high at the time themselves. Kesey was spraypainting designs on the cardboard sleeves that would hold the video cassettes and setting them outside the doorway to dry. Later he would sign each one. It seemed a lively cottage industry. I liked the terms of the transaction, which were straight out of the '60s. No money up front. You ordered the tape, Kesey and company mailed it, and when you received it you sent your payment.

At the farm, Kesey and Ken Babbs, neighbors and close sidekicks since their Stanford days together, got the current bus—son of Furthur, or son of son of Furthur—coughing to life with some shots of starting fluid, and Prankster George Walker drove it creepingly out of its shed. (A trope, it seemed, for the persistence of the '60s in our lives.) We and the Berrys admired its zany, mysterious, brightly painted designs and figures. Kesey circled the bus slowly, pointing out details, presenting with evident pride the vehicle that had come to stand as the single most vivid emblem of his influence on American culture.

A year later, in November 2001, the same bus would bear his body to his memorial service at the McDonald Theater, where he had performed as a child in the 1940s. Once again, for the last time, Ken Kesey was center-stage, this time in a coffin hand-painted in swirling pastels, less vivid but more flowing than the painting on the bus. The theater was packed with more than a thousand people. I squeezed into the balcony, against a wall where I could hear and sometimes see. Musician Mason Williams and friends, stage-right, were playing "Ripple," the great contemporary spiritual written and popularized by the Grateful Dead.

After a while Dave Frohnmayer, president of the University of Oregon, spoke of his long acquaintance with Kesey, remarking on his strength as a collegiate wrestler, his generosity to the university, and his kindness toward the Frohnmayer family. (They lost a college-age daughter some years after the Keseys lost their eldest son Jed, a UO wrestler, when the team bus skidded over a cliff in Washington State.) Frohnmayer assessed Kesey as the single greatest exemplar of the soul and spirit of Oregon. Kesey's agent then spoke, someone read from *Sometimes a Great Notion*, and son Zane Kesey showed a video — as Mason Williams sang "Shall We Gather at the River" — featuring the Reverend Ken "For God's Sake" Kesey, in a dapper black suit and hat, haranguing his flock to abandon drugs and whiskey and all other spirits into the river, the good river, and assuring them that the river would indeed receive them. "We *shall* gather there," assured the Reverend K.

Ken Babbs told of helping to dig the grave the day before. He had decided to scoop one shovelful for every year he had known his friend. Forty-three shovels. Then, that night, he woke up cold and panicked — "Oh my God, it's forty-*four*." Babbs recounted how Kesey would stay after readings to sign books — not just sign, but ornately and uniquely inscribe each one — for every soul who wanted him to. On one occasion he was still signing under a streetlight outside a long-closed bookstore at two o'clock in the morning. Babbs, a man of irrepressibly happy spirit, didn't break down till the end of his talk. He had driven to the farm on a morning soon after Kesey had died and seen there an enormous flock of geese in a field, the most he could remember, and as he drove up they had all lifted off at once. "Sparks Fly Upward," read the marquee outside the McDonald.

Ken Babbs's daughter Rachel led us through "Amazing Grace," then another short reading from *Notion*, and nephew Kit Kesey, manager of the McDonald, said a few words. His uncle had told him, a day or two before he died, "Kit, I'm going to fill that theater for you." As the Grateful Dead's "And We Bid You Goodnight" played over the sound system—*Lay down, lay down and take your rest*—the eight pallbearers got the casket down off the stage, struggling with the considerable load. Then came the most striking moment of the service. Voices called out from around the theater: "Bye, Ken!" "We love you." "See you soon, Ken." The bearers got him up the aisle and into the lobby, where the thick crowd pressed back in silence to let them pass. The bearers secured the casket on a platform on the back of the bus, and the bus pulled away, the bell on its rear-roof tolling.

But a year earlier, during our visit to the farm, there had been no bells tolling and no thoughts of death. In the warmth of the Keseys' barn-become-house, accompanied by several Pranksters and members of the Kesey family, the old friends talked. Wendell Berry observed that of all the Green Bay Packers, only he and Kesey remained married to their wives of that time. The two of them remembered an occasion when Berry had visited the farm on a reading trip. At the end of the visit, Kesey and two Pranksters, as a special gift, had delivered Berry to Eugene not by car but in a drift boat on the Willamette River, making the most of a beautiful day. Kesey, of course, was the skipper. After a leisurely picnic on the river-bank, the group toured the Kesey family dairy. Not once did anyone look at a watch or speak of Berry's flight, he told me later, yet they fetched him to the airport right on time. That way of things working out on the practical level seemingly without thought or concern, he told me, was as characteristic of Kesey's doings as the generosity and style of the gift itself.

Kesey, at sixty-five, was still recognizable as Malcolm Cowley described him in 1960, with "the build of a plunging halfback, big shoulders and a neck like the stump of a Douglas fir." As I watched him, I suddenly understood and vanquished a feeling that had troubled me for decades. I had been one of the many who waited impatiently through the '70s and '80s for a new novel, another major work, and I was one of the many who were disappointed in the books Kesey eventually did produce. Disappointed. As if writing two of the best American novels of the late twentieth century, and boldly lighting our times with his singular verve and enthusiasm, had not been enough. As if Ken Kesey owed me, owed us, when in truth we all owed him.

We ate dinner that evening at two round oak tables. At mine, as Ken Babbs riffed—cheeks flaring, eyes wide and bright, laughing his laugh of absolute commitment to the wonderment of living—the Prankster-in-Chief looked very much the country squire: at home in his chair, pleased with the company, making sure that wineglasses were filled when they needed to be filled and that all present had seconds and a fair shot at thirds of the great slab of salmon Faye Kesey had baked. It was a fine feast, and so was Ken Kesey's extraordinary life, and I am grateful for everything he served.

Wallace Stegner's Hunger for Wholeness

One night years ago as I was rereading some of the essays in *The Sound of Mountain Water*, I heard myself say to my wife, "Wallace Stegner is one of the *wholest* American writers." Marilyn did not reply, as it was two in the morning and she was asleep. I took her rapt silence as affirmation and decided I would try to track down what my remark might mean.

I can't think of another writer who distinguished himself or herself in so many fields of prose: novel, short story, personal essay, memoir, history, biography, literary journalism. Only poetry, it seems, eluded Stegner's pen. He did like verse, though, and when I was around him he frequently quoted lines from Milton, Wordsworth, or his friend Robert Frost, some of which he had carried in memory all the way from his early schooling in the 1910s and '20s. He liked Robinson Jeffers and some contemporary poetry, especially that of Wendell Berry and William Stafford. Once, giddy from having my first essay accepted by *Wilderness* magazine, I told Stegner that I might quit writing poems altogether. "Don't you dare," he said. "It was the poets who led us out of the caves."

Imagine my pleasure, then, when I discovered that Stegner had scribbled a verse or two after all. One day in the 1980s at Stanford University, when I should have been reading student papers, I wandered instead into an unoccupied neighboring office and browsed through a few dusty books. Opening a little volume titled *Historia de España*, copyright 1923, I was shocked to find on the flyleaf the signature of Wallace Stegner, along with "Español 5" and "Universidad de Utah." I leafed ahead and found page after page of penciled Stegner artwork (labeled "futuristic" by the artist) and various marginalia, including two short poems. One of them was a biblical couplet:

Yea verily I say unto you
¿How's your old lady?

The other delivers itself in five snappy lines:

Socrates
Apple crates
Insurance rates
Pair of eights
Soul mates

Unambitious, perhaps, but not the dullest poetry of the early twentieth century.

I can't resist mentioning that on another page I caught young Stegner practicing the *S* in his last name, shaping it something like the G-clef and something like a dollar sign. He sensed, perhaps, that in the life ahead he might need to be signing his name a lot. I also found three pairs of seeming nonsense words that suddenly came clear as female names written backwards. Whatever Grace Anderson, Nola Cook, and Carol Barclay saw in Stegner, it seems likely that Stegner saw poetry in them.

But the wholeness of Wallace Stegner I value most is not a matter of poetry and not merely a matter of his versatility. It has to do with what he put into his prose and what he put into himself in the course of his eighty-four years. Marilyn and I had the good fortune to live on the Stegner homeplace, in Los Altos Hills, California, for five years in the 1980s while I was teaching undergraduate poetry workshops and freshman English at Stanford. We rented a small, redwood-sided cottage that had been Stegner's writing studio in the 1950s, and we worked off the rent doing various chores of gardening and maintenance around the small acreage of grass, native oaks, and flower beds. In this way we came to know Wallace and

Mary Stegner pretty well. In the course of a week I usually worked several afternoon hours with Wally, who had quit teaching more than a decade earlier. He spent his forenoons writing—he created *Crossing to Safety*, his last novel, in those years—and after lunch and a brief nap was ready to get after whatever needed doing outdoors.

He was tall, silver-haired, and usually smiling, and in his smile, the lines of his age all participating, you could see the boy he had been on the Saskatchewan plains, in Salt Lake City, and elsewhere in the North American West. Marilyn, and other female acquaintances as well, found very fetching a certain sly sparkle in his eyes.

"So he stands out among older men?" I asked her once.

"No," she replied. "He stands out among *men*."

Wally relished his work. He moved from task to task around the place—weeding, pruning, spading, painting a downspout, trapping the insufferable gophers—in a kind of loping shuffle, torso tilted forward, feet keeping close to the ground. It was eager and careful at the same time. Mary didn't much care for it. "Wally," I heard her tell him once, "you shuffle along as if you were late for a train. Why can't you walk more like John?" I proceeded in silence with my errand of the moment, suddenly delighted with the dignity of my gait, grateful that there was at least one walk of life in which I might serve as a model for Wallace Stegner.

He got a lot done in an afternoon, shuffling in that deliberate hurry from orchids to carport to pool to woodpile, and at something like the same pace he got a lot done in his lifetime, too—shuttling around the West as a boy, awakening in his teens and moving on through schools and teaching jobs to the work of writing, his index fingers punching the keys of his manual typewriter every day from sunup to noon. From sentence to sentence and page to page, he turned out more than thirty books by the time he was done. Wallace Stegner had an ego, he enjoyed the attention he came to receive, the praise for his writing and teaching and environmentalism, the major honors and prizes, but it wasn't those that kept him punching the keys. He relished his work. Even as he was pushing eighty, nothing left to prove, every morning he was hungry to pick up the typescript pages on the desk in his study and add a few more.

His hunger started young. Listen to the beginning of his brief essay "The Sound of Mountain Water":

> I discovered mountain rivers late, for I was a prairie child, and knew only flatland and dryland until we toured the Yellowstone country in 1920, loaded with all the camp beds, auto tents, grubboxes, and auxiliary water and gas cans that 1920 thought necessary. Our road between Great Falls, Montana, and Salt Lake City was the rutted track that is now Highway 89. Beside a marvelous torrent, one of the first I ever saw, we camped several days. That was Henry's Fork of the Snake.
>
> I didn't know that it rose on the west side of Targhee Pass and flowed barely a hundred miles, through two Idaho counties, before joining the Snake near Rexburg; or that in 1810 Andrew Henry built on its bank near modern St. Anthony the first American post west of the continental divide. The divide itself meant nothing to me. My imagination was not stretched by the wonder of the parted waters, the Yellowstone rising only a few miles eastward to flow out toward the Missouri, the Mississippi, the Gulf, while this bright pounding stream was starting through its thousand miles of canyons to the Columbia and the Pacific.
>
> All I knew was that it was pure delight to be where the land lifted in peaks and plunged in canyons, and to sniff air thin, spray-cooled, full of pine and spruce smells, and to be so close-seeming to the improbable indigo sky. I gave my heart to the mountains the minute I stood beside this river with its spray in my face and watched it thunder into foam, smooth to green glass over sunken rocks, shatter to foam again.

The piece goes on for two more paragraphs of river description and contemplation, paragraphs as lyrical as any Wallace Stegner wrote. They are the payoff of the piece, and they pay handsomely. If I had camped by that river as a kid and written a short essay about it later in life, I wouldn't have included the preliminary details of the river's history because I very likely wouldn't have known them. I might have mentioned the continental divide but probably not the source and length and terminus of Henry's Fork—again, I probably wouldn't have known or sought that information. In short, I would have written, in prose or in verse, a lyric poem about my first encounter with a mountain river. And maybe that suggests one reason why Wallace Stegner didn't write verse. For the poet, if I may overgeneralize to make a point, the lyric moment is consuming and aesthetically sufficient unto itself. For Stegner, the lyric moment may be intense but is never sufficient. In his writing you will find songful passages of exquisite grace, but you will not find personal rhapsody without a context of geography and history. The merely personal present is not, for Stegner, the stuff of which literature is made.

Note the rhetorical strategy by which he informs the reader of what, as an adult writer, he has informed himself. The information is carried in a string of negative expressions, a technique he used frequently. I call it the informational negative:

I didn't know that it rose on the west side of Targhee Pass. . . .

The divide itself meant nothing to me. My imagination was not stretched by the wonder of the parted waters. . . .

All I knew was that it was pure delight. . . .

"All I knew," of course, works two ways: a full cup to the enthralled eleven-year-old, but only half a cup to the adult remembering and writing the experience. And only half a cup, I think that writer would argue, to anyone who would know and write of the American land in its wholeness.

———

Let me enlarge my point by turning to one of Wallace Stegner's master-pieces. *Wolf Willow* is an account of return and remembering, a midlife putting together of the place and culture he came from. He announces the project of the book on the first page: "That block of country between the Milk River and the main line of the Canadian Pacific, and between approximately the Saskatchewan-Alberta line and Wood Mountain, is what this book is about. It is the place where I spent my childhood. It is also the place where the Plains, as an ecology, as a native Indian culture, and as a process of white settlement, came to their climax and their end."

The personal reference is one short sentence between two long ones. Autobiography, Stegner is signaling the reader, is only one element in a much larger story. The first few pages of the book are mostly history, more human than natural; he shows us the past he didn't come from—the gun-toting culture of horse-opera movies—and the immense Plains landscape that did indeed form his soul and character. The present-time narrative of his return to that country as a man in his forties begins unobtrusively. Not until page six does the narrator "poke the car tentatively eastward . . . from Medicine Hat, easing watchfully back into the past." As he homes in on the town of Whitemud, the house and play-haunts of his childhood, he sizes memory against present perception, and the personal narrative expands. He is literally re-membering, piecing together his past, trying to make it whole in his present mind. The process culminates, not as he views the house his father built or the businesses on Main Street, but when he identifies a pervasive smell that captures him beside the Whitemud River. It is wolf willow, a native riparian bush. Stegner makes his past whole by exercising our oldest sense:

> For a few minutes, with a handful of leaves to my nose, I look
> across at the clay bank and the hills beyond where the river loops
> back on itself, enclosing the old sports and picnic ground, and
> the present and all the years between are shed like a boy's clothes
> dumped on the bathhouse bench. . . . A contact has been made.

. . . A hunger is satisfied. The sensuous little savage that I once was is still intact inside me.

For many writers in this age of memoir, amplifications of this realization would have constituted the bulk and thrust of the story: I have returned, I have remembered who I was and now I know better who I am. But for Stegner the personal is not sufficient. This realization comes in chapter one, the first of nineteen plus an epilogue. The next two chapters amplify the personal story, but in the following nine he progresses to the larger weave in which his family's life is only one thread. He gives the history of the town and region — the history that he did not receive as a child, because it had not been recorded or thought important and because the white-settlement phase of it was only beginning in 1914 when his family arrived. The middle-aged writer is regretful, even resentful, over what he missed as a boy. In chapter nine the informational negative introduces paragraph after paragraph, ringing like a litany:

> The very richness of that past as I discover it now makes me irritable to have been cheated of it then.

> All of it was legitimately mine, I walked that earth, but none of it was known to me.

> I wish we had known it. I wish we had heard of the coming of the Sioux, when they rode northward after annihilating Custer's five troops on the Little Big Horn, a whole nation moving north, driving the buffalo before them, and with the soldiers from every army post between Canada and Texas on their track.

> I knew the swallows and muskrats, and was at ease with them. . . . But Time, which man invented, I did not know. I was an unpeopled and unhistoried wilderness, I possessed hardly any of the associations with which human tradition defines and enriches itself.

In an interview recorded in 1987, Stegner likened the absence of those associations to a deficiency disease, a condition that stunts the human spirit as malnutrition stunts the body. But he refused to remain stunted. To heal means to make whole, and Wallace Stegner, deprived of wholeness as a child, would follow his hunger and heal himself in a singular and prodigious way. He made himself into the Herodotus of the Cypress Hills, unearthing and imagining and writing the very history he had wanted as a boy.

Stegner said, characteristically, that the main task of *Wolf Willow* was history; autobiography and fiction were adjuncts to the historical account. I would put it a different way. I see the book as shaped and powered by the needs of knowledge seeking its wholeness. Personal memory comes more or less to completion in the first three chapters. But personal memory — as the author remarks several times in the book, and as any writer of memoir knows — is uneven and unreliable, and even in its wholeness is insufficient. And so he augments personal memory with the collective memory of history, but even that larger memory is limited and insufficient — insufficient, at least, to a writer of Wallace Stegner's hunger. He ends the book with the epic novella "Genesis" and its sequel story "Carrion Spring," extending his act of memory beyond the horizon of personal and historical fact into the further realization of fictional creation, and a book that would have been ample as a memoir and history becomes something more, the very most its author could make it — a full-immersion baptism in the times and landscape that made him, one of the great acts of knowing in the American literature of place.

"I thought I could get more truth into a slightly fictionized story of the winter that killed the cattle industry on the northern plains than I could into any summary," Stegner remarked in his essay "On the Writing of History." Without "Genesis," a reader of *Wolf Willow* would know *about* the harsh climate of the Canadian plains; with it, he knows that brutal cold in his bones and blood. With "Carrion Spring" he knows from a woman's perspective the isolated home imprisonment of that same awful winter. Both stories are fundamentally about cooperation: a band of buckaroos on roundup suddenly must work together to survive; a newly wedded husband and wife struggle to settle their claims on place, culture, and each other. Both reflect another form of wholeness Wallace Stegner hungered for—the wholeness of community, including the community of marriage and family. By and large, acts of individual heroism did not interest him as much as acts of individuals working and neighboring and loving together.

That was the wholeness he wished for his mother, who had the character and skills to be a sticker, a community builder, but was married to a man who did not. "How hungry you were!" Stegner addresses her in "Letter, Much Too Late." "How you would have responded to the opportunities ignored by so many who have them!" And in these words, of course, his own hunger as a boy is spoken, the hunger he remembers in *Wolf Willow* as giving him a bolt of joy at the sight of town, "looped in its green coils of river, snug and protected in its sanctuary valley," when the family trekked back from their dryland wheat farm in the fall. Town was school and games and friendship, the post office, travelers from afar. During summers on the homestead—three hundred and twenty acres of wind and grass, bounded by one iron post and three survey stakes—the boy's hunger for human association could express itself only in a passionate regard for the footpaths the family walked into the prairie in their daily living. In the last chapter of *Wolf Willow*, titled "The Making of Paths," Stegner tells of his frustration when other members of the family cut across to the privy from the wrong corner of the house, ignoring the proper trail. "I scuffed and kicked at clods and persistent grass clumps," he writes, "and twisted my weight on incipient weeds and flowers, willing that the trail around the inside of our pasture should be beaten dusty and plain, a worn border to our inheritance."

When three summers of drought did in his father's farming fantasy and set the family on its erratic way again, the eleven-year-old Stegner (soon to see his first mountain river and his first flush toilet) took with him hungers he didn't know he had, hungers of incompleteness that would drive him through a mighty career. But he did leave with one kind of completeness already realized. In six formative years he had come to know intimately the land and life and weather of the Plains. He knew the "pushing and shouldering wind, a thing you tighten into as a trout tightens into fast water . . . a grassy, clean, exciting wind, with the smell of distance in it, and in its search for whatever it is looking for it turns over every wheat blade and head, every pale primrose, even the ground-hugging grass." He knew the circling horizon always miles away, "as clean a line as the nearest fence." And he knew the immense sky, "alive with navies of cumuli, fair-weather clouds, their bottoms as even as if they had scraped themselves flat against the flat earth."

In the 1987 interview, Stegner said he could draw pictures of Plains wildflowers he hadn't seen since he was ten. He knew the particulars of that country, and he knew its changefulness, the way tornadic storms could boil up in a blue-black sky. But he also knew, beyond its things and motions, the country's elemental permanence — disk of earth and bowl of sky, exact circle of horizon, segmented lines of fence and roadway. "A country of geometry," he calls it in *Wolf Willow*, a "Euclidean perfection." It is the paradox of that landscape to be simultaneously empty and archetypally whole, and human presence there is paradoxical as well — a person is on the one hand tiny, on the other "as sudden as an exclamation mark, as enigmatic as a question mark. . . . At noon the total sun pours on your single head; at sunrise or sunset you throw a shadow a hundred yards long."

Stegner argued in his essay "Ansel Adams and the Search for Perfection" that the Sierra Nevada, particularly Yosemite, had taught Adams how to see and made him the photographer he was. It may be as reasonable to argue that the Northern Plains taught Wallace Stegner how to see and made him the writer he was. Surely a writer under the influence of that entire and empty landscape is likely to look outward, beyond himself, for his completeness. Such a writer is likely to know the singularity of particular things and creatures lit by a sun that shines in summer from four o'clock in the morning until nine at night. He will be interested in community, a student of how people get by together, but he will also be self-sufficient. He is likely to carry within him a sense of possibility as immense as the land around him. And he may want to make a mark — a question mark, an exclamation mark, a mark perhaps like the pathways that fired his young mind. It may be a seemly mark, but not a small one. An artist whose mind comes to light in that expansive space will be no miniaturist.

"I may not know who I am," Stegner writes in *Wolf Willow*, "but I know where I am from." That well-known comment may be misleading. Wallace Stegner knew very well who he was — knew himself better than anyone else in my experience — and he knew who he was precisely because he knew where he was from, including its beauties and powers as well as its strict limits. In one of his last essays he writes, "There is something about exposure to that big country that not only tells an individual how small he is, but steadily tells him who he is. I have never understood identity problems." And he goes on to write: "I knew well enough who, or *what*, I was, even if I didn't matter. As surely as any pullet in the yard, I was a target, and I had better respect what had me in its sights."

A target. The pullet in the yard had been the target of a ferruginous hawk dropping out of an empty sky just a few yards from young Stegner, an event he witnessed several times. But what in that immensity had *him* in its sights? His sense of vulnerability may have had to do with being a sickly child whose mind was two years ahead of his body in school, and who grew up, in the adult writer's words, "hating my weakness and cowardice." It surely had to do with being the son of an angry father who once broke the boy's collar bone with a stick of firewood. Waiting out a cyclone lashed to a survey stake in a one-foot hole in the prairie may have contributed as well. But in the 1987 interview Stegner put the sense of being a target in a different light. He spoke of the uncanny doubleness one feels beneath that enormous sky, a sense "of observing everything else the way God may be observing you."

Wallace Stegner didn't refer to God very often. I don't know what God meant to him. But I suspect that the sense of being transcendently observed would come easily in the Plains country, and with it a sense of being inevitably known, of being a question mark unable to hide, and I suspect that such an awareness contributed considerably to the healthy hunger of Stegner's eighty-four years. A targeted man, a man in the sights of a power he respects and fears and loves, is likely to work as hard and as well and as long as he can.

Talking once with a group of Greek writers about having grown up without history, Stegner was surprised to hear from some of the Greeks that they envied him. Their rich and lengthy past felt like no blessing, they said, in the diminished present of their culture. "But I envied them more than they envied me," Stegner writes, "for what they had was what I had spent my life hopelessly trying to acquire."

A targeted man might look at his life that way, I suppose, but the statement is hopelessly inaccurate. Stegner did indeed grow up, as he puts it in *Wolf Willow*, in a "dung-heeled sagebrush town on the disappearing edge of nowhere, utterly without painting, without sculpture, without architecture, almost without music or theater, without conversation or languages or bookstores, almost without books." He was indeed "charged with getting in a single lifetime, from scratch, what some people inherit as naturally as they breathe air." And get it he did. There was nothing hopeless or halfway about the lifelong acquisition of wholeness he embarked upon once his hunger took hold of him. In his senior year of high school he shot up six inches, finding himself suddenly as big as his classmates. And in his inner life, his cultivation of himself, you get the feeling he took off at the same rate and scarcely slowed.

Hunger is a powerful need, and it can be a powerful asset. Ask any writer, any artist, if he does his best work after a big meal or before. Ask any mountain lion. Wallace Stegner knew the value of learning and training and opportunities for the soul's expansion, and sought them as energetically as he did, precisely because they had been unavailable to him for much of his youth. Few writers now, I would hazard to say, grow up deprived in that way. The situation of most American authors coming of age in the early twenty-first century varies sharply from Stegner's in the early twentieth. There are and there always will be exceptions, but by and large writers today come up well schooled, richly provided with books and museums and performance halls, hundreds of college creative writing programs waiting to nurture and unfold their talents and eventually perhaps to employ them.

And what has this meant for our literature? It's burgeoning, certainly. A great plenty is being written and published, and some of that plenty is good. I have to wonder, though, if contemporary literature isn't suffering in some ways from a lack of hunger in its creators. Where is the ambition, for instance, to be knowledgeable of history and geography and other fields beyond the increasingly specialized craft and criticism of creative writing? Where is the desire to write well in several genres? Where is the awareness of tradition—of one's place in what Stegner called "the great community" of recorded human experience? And where, especially, is the writing that seeks its wholeness outward, recognizing that personal rapture and private torment are insufficient material for the making of literature? It was Wallace Stegner's project to understand himself in the context of his world. Increasingly, it seems, it is the project of contemporary writing to understand the world—or fail to understand it—in the context of the self.

No doubt I am exaggerating to make a point. Today's literature is by no means entirely self-referential or self-enclosed. And I certainly don't wish to glorify cultural deprivation, and repackage the destructive myth that art, in order to be authentic, must be the product of hardship. Talent finds its way, whether born with a silver pen in its hand or with dung on its heels, and our time has its share of talent. But talent, even genius, does not make a writer. Neither does the capacity to emote. Literature must be more than self-expression. "If a writer has only himself to say,"

Stegner remarked and wrote more than once, "his work will be kind of thin."

That is an old-fashioned idea, and it came from an old-fashioned man. "I really don't belong in the twentieth century," Stegner said in conversation with Richard Etulain. "My demands upon life are nineteenth-century demands." Elsewhere he worried that "the principles of restraint, proportion, and a wide representation of all kinds of life — the principles I have tried to live and write by — have all been overtaken and overwhelmed." His concern has greater justification now than when he first expressed it in the 1970s. As book publishing in America becomes a subsidiary business of corporate media conglomerates, the sensationalism of sex and violence that dominates film, television, and video games increasingly drives the book market as well. Many publishers have abdicated their traditional sense of responsibility to the culture, paying huge advances for loud, flashy, and often poorly written novels and for mediocre nonfiction by or about celebrities. The more modest but well-crafted books that do get published are kept in print, if at all, through the life support of small-batch print-on-demand.

And yet, for all that, a book as quiet and quirky as *Wolf Willow* is in print today and has hardly been out of print in the near half-century since its initial publication. *Crossing to Safety*, Stegner's late novel on the very unsensational subject of friendship — another kind of wholeness he favored, along with marriage for the long term — sold thirty-five thousand hardback copies and countless paperbacks since it appeared in 1987. Fifteen years after his death, most of the major books Wallace Stegner wrote are now in print in one edition or another. When I see him in my mind these days, he's smiling, and maybe not only with self-satisfaction. Maybe his own late-life and posthumous success would convince even him that there remains a sizable audience for old-fashioned books that bring into focus what is worthy and enduring in human experience. The wholest writers are those with a complex sense of responsibility to history, community, nature, and culture — to values that transcend their private epiphanies and miseries, to whatever it is that holds them in its sights and demands the most of them. Wallace Stegner was that kind of writer. For sixty years, every morning till noon, he extended a carefully considered pathway out of the nineteenth century through the broad terrain of modern American life. That path, inconspicuous but clearly defined, democratic but always demanding, is one of the routes most likely to lead us to a future we want to inhabit.

"Creative Nonfiction"
and the Province of Personal Narrative

There's a story my mother used to tell about me, even occasionally in her last years, when her memory was sliding away in a slow avalanche. Once in the 1950s, when we were living in the semi-rural Maryland outskirts of Washington, D.C., our cat brought a maimed bird to the door. My mother scolded the cat and grieved for the bird, the story goes, until I came to the door behind her, six or seven years old, and pronounced, "Mother, it's a cat's *nature* to hunt birds."

My mother would tell me the story and ask, "Do you remember that?"

"I remember," I'd tell her. Memory was a thing of moments for my mother near the end of her life. It was good to be able to share them.

In truth, however, I told her a lie. I didn't then and don't now remember saying those words. I don't remember what kind of bird it was, or what the cat looked like. I have only the vaguest image of the entryway to that house, only a shadowy recollection of my mother's appearance at that time in our lives. I assured her that I remembered the experience; in truth, I remembered her telling the story about me over the years. I remembered being remembered. The story has replaced the event. The story has become the truth, as far as anyone in the world knows the truth.

Earlier in her life, I think my mother used to tell the story in greater detail. There was more about the poor bird, more about my manner and admonishing tone. Did she tell the experience exactly as it had happened? I doubt it. Surely she elaborated, at least slightly. Surely she shaped up my pronouncement, editing for effect, embellishing perhaps, when recounting the incident, over drinks, to family and friends. It was a good little story, and few can resist the impulse to make a good story better.

Actually, none of us can, because memory itself alters and cuts and elaborates our stories. There's an image I've had drifting around the threshold of awareness my entire life, a memory that became very important to me in my mid-forties when I set out to write a memoir about my mother and my own childhood and early adulthood. The event I think I remember occurred at night, maybe when I was two years old. The sense of it is vague, but I believe it occurred in my mother's arms. I seem to remember the warmth and gentle pressure of arms and breast. And I seem to recall a voice speaking, drawing my awareness out into the world. The words are indistinct, but I hear the murmuring of the voice like a stream moving over stones, the syllables all dissolved in the lilt and whisper of their flow. Maybe it was her blood and breathing I was hearing, maybe it wasn't language at all.

But it's the stars I remember best, or believe I remember. It's the stars I think of as my first seeing. Maybe my mother was talking about them, crooning about them. I saw a scatter of light above me, and it was in seeing that scatter of light that I first distinguished a world separate from me and a me separate from the world. I think of it as my second birth, as profound as my first — more profound, in a way, because it was the birth of consciousness, of the point of view I would come to know as myself, more *me* than arms or legs.

There are other details of that moment that I want to say I remember — that the night air was warm and soft on my face, that the stars looked cold somehow, that crickets were sounding, that a dog barked. But how could I at two years old have been aware of anything I could identify and remember as the sound of crickets? A barking dog, maybe, because we had a dog, but crickets? And what did I know of the sensation of cold that I could transfer to the stars? Surely my imagination has invented these details, remembering them into the recollection of voice and stars in order to make the scene more vivid, more immediate. I'm a writer, after all, and I have a writer's instinct for artifice. I want the scene to be vivid and immediate for the reader, and that artifice may be only an extension of a deeper, pre-verbal artifice. Something in my psyche wants to make the scene vivid and immediate for *me*, the me who distantly remembers it. Memory itself is a fabricator, a spinner of yarns, a poet and a liar.

As I exercised memory in writing my book I became very interested in how it works. Scientists for decades have been trying to discover the sites in the brain where memories are stored. They are finding that certain structures and regions of the brain are critical in various ways to the functioning of memory, but it seems there are no storage sites per se. When we remember an experience, the brain does not retrieve a record of it in the way of a computer retrieving information from its memory banks. There is no record. The brain *re-creates* the experience, conjuring images out of labyrinthine loopings of neurons firing in several regions of the brain in a complex pattern similar to the one triggered by the original experience.

The re-creation is not a photocopy. According to the neurobiologist Gerald Edelman, there are ten billion neurons in the human cerebral cortex, and more potential connections between those neurons than there are subatomic particles in the entire estimated physical universe. It is a system of near-infinite complexity, a system that seems designed for revision as much as for replication, and revision unquestionably occurs. Details from separate experiences weave together, so that the conscious mind thinks of them as having happened together. The actual year or season or time of day shifts to a different one. Many details are lost, usually in ways that serve the self in its present situation, not the self of ten or twenty or forty years ago when the remembered event took place. But even the fresh memory, the "original," is not reliable in a documentary sense. It happens all the time that two trustworthy eyewitnesses to a recent incident give widely divergent accounts. We remember not the story of what happened but always *a* story, a version, an account that fits our present understanding of life and helps us get on with it. That story is subject to unconscious revision over time. The current draft becomes for us *the* story, the vague recollection or clear and certain memory we would swear to.

Memory, then, is less a record of the past than an evolving myth of understanding the psyche spins from its engagement with life. I mean "myth" in its two opposed senses — a story so true you live your life by it, and an untruth presented as fact. Subjects in psychological tests can easily be induced to remember things that didn't happen. When a subject is asked, after watching a film of an accident, "How fast do you think the cars were going when they smashed into each other?" he is likely to remember broken glass. If asked without "smashed" or "fast" in the question, he is much less likely to remember broken glass. (There is no broken glass in the film.) In another experiment, conducted by Elizabeth Loftus at the University of Washington, kids and adults too can be prompted to remember having once been lost in a mall and very frightened about it. Memory is capable not only of revision but of outright invention.

Major memories as well as trivial ones can be invented. Someone who recalls being sexually abused as a child may remember and recount the violation in vivid detail. The violation may or may not have occurred. Without a witness, there is often no way to determine the truth. (Even a confession is not necessarily reliable. False confessions to crimes occur frequently, and not as a result of torture.) Hypnotizing the accuser not only doesn't help, it increases the likelihood of false memory. Hypnotized subjects often remember with great confidence and detail, but it turns out that the hypnotized mind is an even better fabricator than the mind in its ordinary state, and the hypnotized subject is extremely suggestible to intended or unintended cues from the questioner. It is for these reasons that hypnotically "refreshed" testimony, common in years past, is now generally disallowed in most courtrooms.

The stakes are high for those involved in such memory-based disputes, and they are high for writers, too, especially writers of personal narrative. My memories live at the center of my being. My memories are *me*, and if I can't know them to be true, how can I know who I am? How, I had to ask myself as I wrote my book, could I write a memoir if I couldn't trust memory?

I answered the question in three ways. First, I decided to communicate my beliefs and understandings about memory as an intermittent commentary woven throughout the book. Second, when I felt less than certain about a memory that mattered, I acknowledged my uncertainty to the reader. And third, I realized and also acknowledged to the reader that for better or for worse I was writing a *story*, and that story, though it contains history, is not and cannot be synonymous with it.

The Swiss psychologist Jean Piaget once told an interviewer about one of his first conscious experiences. He remembered being pushed in a perambulator by his nanny when she was attacked by a man who wanted her purse. Throughout his youth Piaget recalled the attacker's bearded face, the nanny screaming and scratching his arm, the flash of sun on her parasol as she beat him with it, and other specific details. Later in life, as a young adult, Piaget discovered that the incident he remembered so vividly had never occurred. The nanny had been unaccountably late getting the little boy home and had concocted the tale of the attacker to satisfy the parents. Evidently she was a good storyteller, and little Piaget a receptive listener. Retellings by his parents no doubt further strengthened the details in his memory. His nanny's false alibi became absolute truth to him.

If the nanny and parents had filed a complaint, and if a bearded man with a scratch or two on his arm had been charged with the attack, Piaget's memory might have abetted his nanny's confabulation in perpetrating an injustice. But the needs of art are not the same as the needs of law. If Piaget had never discovered the falsehood of his memory, and if in his forties, say, he had undertaken a memoir of his childhood, that "experience" might have proven very valuable. It might have constellated with other memories in ways that helped him understand his fears, his sense of gender roles and relations, his attitudes toward violence, his sense of security or insecurity. False as history, the story was as true to Piaget as anything that had really happened to him. In terms of his subjective experience it did really happen.

That's the way it may have worked with my own, less dramatic memory. I may never have seen the stars from my mother's arms. It may have been Nanny, the black woman who helped with housekeeping when my brother and I were small, who carried me out and murmured to me. I may have seen not stars but fireflies, which I also remember from an early age. Or the image may have come from a song, a story, from who knows what or where. But what I have, regardless of its origin, is the image. I opened my eyes in my mother's arms and saw the stars, and in that moment I woke to consciousness. I've carried that glimpse for sixty years, and not it alone. In writing my book I found that memory responds to attention — wakened images wake others.

When I was five or so, my mother was trying to explain the West Coast to me, a place called Oregon. I got it that the land went on a long way from where we lived and ended in Oregon, but for some reason, I didn't see it ending at an ocean. I saw mountains, a last solid shore, and then the void of starry space. There was also a recurrent dream I had at that age and older, a nightmare that made me cry out until my mother came to turn on the light and comfort me. No story, just an image. I felt myself floating bodiless among icy stars, a dead soul lost forever from my life.

I still fear the extinction of death, and I've sometimes thought that the glittering sky I saw from my mother's arms somehow branded that fear into me, but it makes no sense. Why would that moment have been fearful? What was death to the I who had just been born beneath those stars? My fear must have come later, from something else, something that turned the stars into cold emblems of death and emptiness.

One of the houses we lived in when I was a schoolboy was a few blocks from the firehouse in Glen Echo, Maryland. The siren was loud, an implacable shriek, and when it went up and leveled off at its highest pitch I would stop everything and wait for it to go back down, because that would mean only a fire. If it didn't go down it meant that Russian missiles were on the way and nothing could stop them, that in a few minutes, along with Congress and the president and my family and friends, I would burn instantly to nothing in a blinding flash. I'd be standing there in my room, then gone. When the siren stayed too many seconds at its top screaming pitch I closed my eyes and *willed* it to go down, then pleaded, hitting my fists against my thighs.

Light, dark. Here, gone. Is that what turned the stars so cold and lonely? Is that what caused me to see an ultimate brink at the end of America? I can't know, but I'm sure of one thing: The starry dark is a deep and primary image for me, a riddle of my being. And so it makes sense that memory should work and worry it, tease it into further images, shape scenes and stories from it, and it makes sense that I should help memory along. The starry dark is integral to the myth of identity that memory weaves within me, and even though memory is a proven liar, I don't believe it's out to trick me or lead me astray. It's my faith that the myth of memory tends toward the truths that I most need to know.

And so, I wrote my book, published as *Looking After: A Son's Memoir*. I tried to remember the boy and young man I had been. I tried to understand how we had gotten split up and how we might get back together. I tried to remember my mother as I had known her throughout my life. I tried to discover what she had meant to me in life and what she meant to me in death. I started with what I recalled and wrote my way into what I didn't. I wrote about real people, real events; and I heightened scenes with sensory details that may have come from memory but just as probably from imagination. I added crickets and barking dogs. I changed the location of certain scenes. I put into mouths — my mother's, my wife's, my own — language never spoken, and put it within quotation marks. I don't remember exact wordings from ten, twenty, or forty years ago. But I remember the persons, I remember some of their habits of speech, I remember the sense and emotional tenor of particular conversations, and so I re-created those conversations in the spirit of truth.

Truth means conformity to fact, but it also means fidelity, or faithfulness. As a writer of personal narrative I owe fidelity to facts. I gather all I can find, rubbing each for its full gleam and color. Each is an element of the story I need to tell. But I also owe fidelity to the unrealized wholeness of the story, the wholeness of which clearly remembered events form only a part. I owe fidelity to what memory can't provide, and how can I possibly practice that faith except by following, in the spirit of truth, the stuttering, devious pencil I hold in my hand?

The nature writer John Burroughs once wrote, "It was not till I got home that I really went to Maine, or the Adirondacks, or to Canada. Out of the chaotic and nebulous impressions which these expeditions gave me, I evolved the real experience." It is the writer's power (and his plight as well) that the real experience occurs not as it happens but back in his study as he writes it. That power is essential to the writing of memoir, and it is easy to abuse. In his study, Burroughs says, he "compels that vague unconscious being within me, who absorbs so much and says so little, to unbosom himself at the point of a pen." If he means that last phrase as a joke, it's a serious joke. The process does involve compulsion.

As I wrote my book there were parts of the story I wanted to leave to my vague unconscious being within, because they didn't show me as I like to be seen. I was far from a perfect caregiver for my mother in her last years. I hurried her when she couldn't hurry, I was impatient with her memory lapses, I cut off conversations, I spent too much of our time together in an irritable funk. There were moments when I wished she would just go ahead and die. The point of the pen must demand an account of those moments too. It must require, at a minimum, the fullest truth memory can provide — memory the self-serving, memory the liar. If the memoirist's task is to bring into being a myth of identity, he must also vet that myth with an honest interrogation.

He must recognize, too, that there are certain absences the pen cannot fill. In my book I recall a scene from my eighth or ninth year when my mother said something very hurtful to me. I remember clearly the look of her face, her posture, the hallway just outside my bedroom where we were standing—the hardwood floor, the dead moths in the overhead light. And I remember—can still feel—the crumpling pain her remark gave me, how it contracted my whole being. But I absolutely do not remember what she said, and in this instance, because the experience was and remains so charged, I did not feel I could put words into her mouth. If I had remembered even the gist of what she said, I might have imagined language for it, but the memory blockage was too complete. It is also entirely possible that she said nothing of the intensely emotional weight I recall, that my memory has fabricated that. In either case, the spirit of truth had too little to work with.

Honorable writers and readers will differ, of course, on how much and what kinds of fabrication are legitimate in memoir. But most would agree, I hope, that the writer must not knowingly distort the lives and character of persons as he has known them, and that he must not knowingly misrepresent his own life or character. In one celebrated instance, a memoir about overcoming a life of addiction and depravity, the author wrote that he had been in jail more than once for up to three months at a time. In fact, he had never been in police custody at all for more than a few hours. Many other of the book's facts and characterizations turned out to be false. That isn't a case of fabricating in the spirit of truth; it is fabricating to self-dramatize. An honest writer can't do that. You can't knowingly distort experience to make your misadventures more harrowing than they were, and you, therefore, by implication, all the more heroic for having overcome them. I hope readers of memoir will care to distinguish that sort of gross, self-aggrandizing falsification from the smaller liberties I have defended as necessary to the telling of a truthful story.

At the point of a pen, however, I must confess what might seem a larger license that I once took. Some years ago I wrote an essay about the clearcutting of old-growth forest, drawing on my experience as a backpacker, an environmentalist, and a former logger. The first nine sections make clear that on ecological and aesthetic grounds I'm against clearcutting as it's been practiced in the Northwest, that I'm for a less profligate, more selective use of the forest. In the tenth and final section I pose a different view, spoken in a particular place and time by a particular logger. I depict the man and his opinion with respect and a measure of sympathy. I acknowledge that his view and the opposing view of contemporary environmentalists both have evidence to support them. In the end I argue that the land itself is the most objective and persuasive evidence, and that the condition of logged-over land in our national forests tilts strongly against widespread clearcutting. (I won't quote the passage here because the essay, "Cuttings," is included in this book.)

The man I briefly picture in this passage is fictitious. Drawing on what I clearly remembered — the very real qualities of many of the men I worked with, the remarks of several of them, the place and weather in which many conversations took place — I fabricated a composite man, stood him in the morning rain, put language in his mouth, and analyzed his apocryphal comment for signs of his mind and heart. I did this because I wanted to suggest to the environmentalists in my audience that economy needs to be considered alongside ecology in the timber debate; that nothing is gained by blaming or condescending to those who work, or worked, in the woods for a living; and that we who use the materials they produce are trapped with them in a polarized discourse, implicated, together with the land itself, in a tragedy. I felt I could convey this better in a narrative vignette than I could in expository argument, because narrative, with sensory particulars, awakens in the reader a livelier attention. I wrote the passage in search of a wholer truth than I had been hearing in the public debate in the early 1990s. It felt true to me as I wrote it, and it feels true to me now.

I wouldn't have created that man if I had been writing journalism. I expect the journalist, including me when I'm writing as one, to present as historically real only those persons and events he knows to be real, and to present them and their comments as accurately as possible. But I wasn't writing journalism. I was attempting a personal essay — a piece of literary art, I like to think—and the essayist, like the memoirist, can and must be more than a chronicler of observed events. He must imagine his experience as thoroughly as he can, and by that I mean not to make it unreal but to make it more real. Like writers of memoir, the essayist bears true witness by seeking to embody in images as well as in thought-at-a-distance the experience that has engaged him.

But if it's permissible for an essayist to invent a character and a conversation, what's to keep him from inventing an entire narrative? What indeed. One of George Orwell's best essays, "A Hanging," from his years in the 1920s as a British magistrate in Burma, is a closely described first-person account of a condemned man's execution. It turns mainly on two seemingly trivial incidents. As the prisoner and his handlers approach the gallows, a dog prances up and leaps to lick the man's face, horrifying everyone. Orwell gets the dog under control, then watches from behind as the man, walking again, steps deftly around a puddle in his path. Those actions, precisely rendered in vivid plain-style prose—the kind of language I urge on all my writing students—induce in Orwell a revelatory flash in which he sees "the mystery, the unspeakable wrongness, of cutting a life short when it is in full tide."

Rather, I should say, they induce that realization in the narrator of the story. According to Bernard Crick, an Orwell biographer and the introducer of the Penguin edition of his selected essays, it is unlikely that Orwell ever attended a hanging, in Burma or anywhere else. (For those who know the essays, there's a better-than-even chance that he never shot an elephant, either.) Has George Orwell, much vaunted for his frank honesty, foisted fiction upon us in the guise of an essay? Has he sold his readers down the river?

Not this one. Orwell may have fabricated more broadly—an entire, essay-length scene—than the writer of the regrettable addiction memoir, and more broadly than I would do, but in no way did he fabricate to aggrandize himself. The very strength of the essay is the complete implication of the narrator in the untenable, dehumanizing brutality of imperial governance. He comes off no better (somewhat worse, rather, since he seems an intelligent and sensitive man) than the gruff, stiff-upper-lipped superintendent he works for and the co-opted Burmese toadies — one showing off his classy European cigarette case — who suck up to them both. Everyone involved, Orwell shows, is corrupted (or jailed and liable to be hanged) by the enterprise of empire. The essay virtually breathes the spirit of truth. From his experience in Burma Orwell had something to say, and he used his narrative imagination to make a far more compelling statement than would have been possible journalistically or in an argumentative essay. He takes us beyond information into a truthful *imagination* of empire.

In short, Orwell earns his authority. The writer of the addiction memoir does not. Alarms go off in the very first scene, in which our hero sits slumped in a commercial airliner, unaccompanied, semi-conscious, a hole in his nose, blood and vomit soaking his shirtfront. How often have you noticed such a fellow traveler on your flight? Certain critics and bloggers, it turns out, raised questions about the memoir when it first was published, well before its sales went nova after Oprah Winfrey anointed it on her TV show.

I think most good readers, like those critics and bloggers, are capable of discerning for themselves when they are being jobbed by an author. And the reader, after all, does bear some responsibility in the matter. A memoir or narrative essay is not a nature trail, with paved walkways, explanatory placards, a map to guide you, and an attentive ranger to see to your needs. When you open a good book you enter a wilderness, and a wilderness, by definition, can bewilder. You can get lost in there. You may see things that only seem to be, as well as things that definitively are. When you come out of it, you may wonder about what you have seen. It may occur to you, for instance, after a few readings of "A Hanging," that the dog — the only nonhuman creature in the story and the only one that responds humanely to the grim proceedings, who appears in not one, not two, but in three crucial moments — is so apt, so perfectly fitted as a foil to the needs of the narrative, so *necessary*, that George Orwell the writer was mighty lucky that this particular dog was there in the prison compound with George Orwell the magistrate and acted exactly as it did. Mighty lucky.

Though "A Hanging" is always anthologized as an essay, I don't know if Orwell or his publisher ever claimed a particular genre for it. In correspondence Orwell referred to another great Burma piece, "Shooting an Elephant," as a "sketch," which suggests an interesting question. Do we expect other kinds of artists to toe the line between fiction and nonfiction? In which genre, for instance, should we place Van Gogh's *Starry Night*? I'm quite sure I've never with my own eyes seen stars as large and as engrossed in such swirling light as Vincent painted. Did he really see them that way, or did he make them up?

The question is laughable. Why then is it so deadly serious to so many when it comes to literary nonfiction?

Part of the problem, clearly, is the term "nonfiction" itself. The only genre defined as the negative of another, it is expected to encompass an impossibly expansive array of forms ranging from journalism and history and biography to memoir and personal essay. To further the problem, the latter two forms, and often literary journalism as well, are usually referred to in journals and classrooms as "creative nonfiction." Creative how? a reader might fairly wonder. In what ways and to what extent? May a literary journalist be as "creative" as a memoirist? Abolishing the phrase "creative nonfiction" would be a good first step toward making sense of the genre. "Personal narrative" is a more natural and more apt name for those forms in which an explicit "I" narrates the story. Writing in which we don't expect an "I," or not much of one—reportage, history, biography, formal essays, literary criticism, other expository and argumentative writing—is harder to label. "General nonfiction" is the usual term, and perhaps will have to do.

Or, we could just call all of it, and fiction too, what it essentially is: prose. Within that broad field I see little organic difference between what I do in memoir and narrative essay and what a fiction writer does in novel and short story. Both of us are trying to tell a story we wish and need to tell, using the same technical devices to tell it, and trying to tell it the truest way we can. We do, of course, bear different responsibilities. The fiction writer may create characters, points of view, and narrative events largely from imagination, while the essayist and memoirist must be harnessed to their own points of view and respect the spirit, if not always the letter, of objective truth. But both kinds of work flow from the same storytelling need and desire, the same narrative fountain in the human psyche. As Thomas Hobbes wrote in *Leviathan* (and as is evident in any young child), "Imagination and memory are but one thing, which for diverse considerations hath diverse names."

In either case, working from imagination or working from memory, we are dealing with fabrications of experience, and our original perceptions of experience are themselves fabrications of the nameless flux in which we and our senses are continuously immersed, which we call life and the world. As Oliver Sacks has written, "When we open our eyes each morning, it is upon a world we have spent a lifetime *learning* to see. We are not given the world; we make our world. . . ." The writer is one who trains this necessary making into language, and in that way makes the world again. Through writing and reading he encourages his fabrications of experience; he conditions himself to respond in associations, in images and metaphors, in complexes of thought and feeling, in scenes and narrative lines. Most of us grow richer with these fabrications as we grow older. When I was twenty I wanted to be a writer but thought I had nothing to write about. I misunderstood the problem. I had lots to write—all of us do, at any age—but not yet a sufficient sense of self, not yet the inner means to compose, to *re-member*, my experience. Now, at sixty, I realize I have more to write than I'll ever have time for.

Philosophically, it's arguable that none of the writing we call nonfiction is actually that. In a sense it's all fiction, a word that derives from the Latin *fingere*, which means not only to feign but also to shape or fashion. All writing is shaped and fashioned, all of it feigns to one degree or another, by both conscious and unconscious choice, and most of it comes down to one form or another of storytelling. "What is history," Napoleon is supposed to have said, "but a fable agreed upon?" What is biography but a story — not *the* story — of a human life? What is science but an enlarging suite of stories told by those who study physical being, revised over time under a set of conventions known as the scientific method? Even news journalists, hard though most of them try, are helpless to remove themselves entirely from their pieces, and they betray the true nature of those pieces when they refer to them as "stories."

But I'm content to limit my argument to what I know best. As I wander the continent of creative writing, following such tracks as seem promising, it's clear enough that the regions of memoir and personal essay interblend in a borderland with the regions of short story and novel. They share similar forms of life. They belong to the same natural province. All that separates them is an artificial construction, a stone wall in about the condition Robert Frost depicts in "Mending Wall." There are some who scurry to gather up fallen stones and rebuild the wall. I wish them no ill, but that work doesn't interest me. I like to pass freely among the strewn stones, speaking with fellow writers and readers who are doing the same. None of us is entitled to put up NO TRESPASSING signs, because none of us owns the landscape on either side, and it's the landscape, and the life we find there, that matters.

Memoir, essay, short story, novel. Call it the province of personal narrative. It's a free country. It gets by without government. Write responsibly.

IV

The Wages of Mortality

THE RIVER

In memoriam: September 11, 2001

The cabin where I lived in solitude during the late fall and winter of 2000–
2001 sits in a meadow high on the north side of the steep, forested Rogue
River Canyon, out of sight of the Rogue but looking out on the spacious
sculpturing the river and its tributaries have accomplished through the
ages. The voice of water on boulders and bedrock, its violence muted by
distance to a wind-like whisper, came to me whenever I remembered to
hear it in the brimming silence.

 I had no visitors, no human news. I followed local stories — deer
browsing the meadow, the precise nasal calls of spotted owls, the drifting,
swirling mist that obscured and revealed the green wooded ridges around
me. In the meadow one night I was startled by a muffled impact close by,
then vague wings shouldering away. Another night I heard from the woods
a rasping, screeching, snarling struggle between creatures I couldn't see,
one fighting to take a life, one fighting to keep it. Once at the river I saw an
osprey dive on a green pool and rise with a steelhead writhing in its talons.
I killed two fish myself that day, rapped their heads on a boulder, saw their
violet-green iridescence fade as they quivered to stillness in my hands.

 A month after the September attacks I went back to the cabin to stay
a few days. I fished a little. I sat and walked by the river, letting its fluent
voices stream through me. It flowed in rapids and smooth green slides just
as it had the winter before. The osprey was there, perched on a snag, and
a great blue heron stood straight and still on a rock.

The river gave me comfort, but the river of course cared no more for me, no more for us and our present pain, than it cared for the miners who once shared meals and stories and occasionally murdered one another by its banks, or for the Indians that the miners and cavalry hunted and killed and drove from the land. The Indians' long habitation, their fire smoke rising to a glittering heaven, was no different to the river than the time before, when no human was here to stand on the banks of the green and gliding waters.

Ancestral otters slipped through the currents, much as their descendants do now. Ouzel-like birds dipped into the shallows and out again. Ancient deer stepped carefully down to drink, as in the woods a big cat tensed and watched. From far at sea old salmon arrived, spawned, and left their ruined bodies; in the spring, small salmon rode the river downstream. Creatures died and creatures lived, species of creatures died and lived as the river roared with killing floods, ran thick with torrents of volcanic ash, dwindled in drought to a rank trickle, and freshened again.

Our lives have flowed from exploding stars, from currents of time and gravity beyond our ken. Nothing in Nature can tell us our story, nothing can explain why today some die while others live on, or why we die at all, or live. The river speaks, but not our tongue. It makes itself of snow and rain, it gathers all that it touches and finds its way. In surging falls and deep green pools, in chutes and riffles and silent swirls, it bears us on through winding passages of grace and fury, until once, perhaps, in a stab of sun on streaming water, the entire aching beauty of being comes clear. . . .

And the river—the good, green, terrible river—flows on.

Solitude in a Dry Season

Rogue River Canyon, 1994

June eleventh. Muggy today, high overcast, not as hot as yesterday's clear-sky bake, but stifling. In the afternoon a wind came up, gusting yellowed madrone leaves around the cabin. Down the Meadows trail, I started the doe and one fawn, the fawn still small and spotted but walking like a deer: those deliberate steps, so carefully placed, the arched front leg brought forward with a concurrent thrust of the head. I remember the cool and misty days of early May when she and her twin had just been born, all of a foot and a half tall, and mostly gangly legs at that. At their mother's signal they'd drop and hold dead still in the grass. Where's her twin? And where has the time gone?

———◆———

I'm not doing so well at simplifying my life here. Hard to know what true simplicity might be, but it wouldn't be this unsettled mind of mine, aswarm with noise and little direction. I've stripped away most distractions, simplified my daily routine, but how do I strip down my busy mind? And do I want to?

———◆———

The little squirrel came to the deck this morning and picked up a feather, turning it in his nimble front paws as he chewed the butt end. If you're a squirrel, it seems, you comprehend a thing by biting it. Maybe that's my trouble. This is a writing residency, but I haven't bit in to anything. I need to find my subject and chew it, learn its flavor. Didn't Van Gogh like to eat paint? Thoreau wrote in his *Journal* about gnawing the bone of life. No bite, no write.

———◆———

Driving in with groceries from Grants Pass, almost to the homestead, and *now* he leaps from the left, bounds two tawny seconds ahead of the truck—his tail so long, so hefty, almost touching the grille—and with one cat-glance back veers off the road into tall brush. Truck stopped, me out on the gravel on trembling legs. . . . He's lost himself in the country. "Thanks for letting me see you," I say, my voice unsteady like a spooked boy's. My legs do not stop trembling. I can't see far into the brush where he vanished. I get back in the truck.

———◆———

I love this bird-call quiet of evening, the hot day cooling, last light passing from the crest of Rattlesnake Ridge, the unseen Rogue sending up its whisper from below. The hermit thrush may know simplicity. He sings. How can he know who he is if he doesn't sing? I'm alive in this world, I want to know. I'll be nothing more than a snail someday, a blade of grass. Now, here, is my chance. Sing, damn it, sing!

———◆———

Two pileated woodpeckers this morning, working the snags out back. They didn't fast-hammer like smaller peckers, they *excavated*, their long bills picking and stabbing in unrushed cadence. From time to time one or the other stilled his red and white head and gave a light, rollicking yammer—two young lords at play, certain of their estate. Tree to tree they flew, tapping a while and moving on, each alighting in the shouldering tent of his great black wings.

The fawn insists this morning. With her snout she punches the doe's milk pouch, hard, again, then grabs hold and sucks. I'm here, she says. Give forth! My mother, dead not quite two years, would have loved seeing this. My delight feels half hers, and it comes with a pang.

A hundred and one today, July ninth. Between sporadic breezes, a stillness of heat so solid it seems to hold me upright in my chair. This country's baking hard and brittle, aromatics wafting off pines and manzanita. Why am I here? I keep returning from town with my week's supplies, hot and frazzled and strewn with clutter of mind as I pull up the drive and cut the engine. Out of sorts, I stow food in the cupboards and propane fridge and get the sprinklers going in the garden, collecting my evening ration of mosquito bites. I read the paper by headlamp as I eat a late supper. The next day I've settled in some, but what I'm trying to write—about being here, the feel of solitude, the beauties of each day—won't find a form. Gary Snyder lets the outside in and the inside out through the open windows of his home. Why can't I open my *self* to this wild river canyon with no human neighbors, no lures of electricity, abundant silence, and six and a half months of time? Three and a half. That's what I'm down to.

Now, late afternoon, a stirring on the far side of the blackberry patch. Little bear! He's down low, on his back, stripping berries with paws and snout. Mostly I see only the canes twitching or shaking, an occasional paw. Ah, what a life. This morning I picked a bowl for my cereal. It's his turn now. He's got the far side, I've got the near. Here at Dutch Henry Homestead, the citizens have it all worked out.

Feeling plucky today. Chainsawed in the afternoon, bucking up downed fir and madrone behind the cabin. I like whipping the little Homelite around, letting the saw-chips fly, inhaling whiffs of sapwood fragrance along with a heady dose of two-cycle exhaust. Bracing! I love the smell of chainsaw fumes in the afternoon. It's the best inspiration I've found, and the work is clear and certain — you can see what you're doing, what you've done, what you'll do next.

------◆------

A motion on my left shoulder — I knock a green spider to the deck. A spider, how hideous! Whatever in me fears these critters is quicker than thought. Decked, he tucks into a little ball, himself his own bunker. I take a sliver and prod, hoping I haven't killed him. I poke again and he breaks into a wild spider run, spinning streamers of web, over the edge of the deck and off into air. Not suicide. Survival. Go crazy!

------◆------

The fawn again, trotting behind her mother, her white, black-edged tail held high. Once in May, starting out in the truck, I surprised them. The mother went straight up the rutted road. One of the fawns couldn't keep up, dropped in a curl. The doe nosed her and the three continued uproad. When the mother climbed the yellow clay bank to the right, seeking the trees, one fawn followed. The weaker one tried but her forelegs crumpled beneath her, soft hooves flailing. She tried again and scrabbled up. Whichever I'm seeing now, looks like her twin didn't make it.

------◆------

The robin dips, dips, and on the third dip bills the crawling bug and bolts it with a flourish, head high! The quiet, the light, the nature of this place — what I'm writing is fine but it's not what I need to write. What I need is here, somewhere, sleeping like the bats in the cedar-shake roof.

THE WAGES OF MORTALITY

On the trail up from a splash in the river I got something about simplicity. I was parched from the climb, lightheaded, my thoughts ahead of me on cold water in a blue plastic tumbler, the La-Z-Boy chair. My thoughts these days haze minutes ahead or years behind. I thought of my mother, at sixty-one, twenty-five years ago, trekking doggedly behind me up a steep Olympic Peninsula trail. Today I stopped on my Rogue River trail, dizzy a little, my thoughts homing in to what I was—heaving lungs, aching knees, familiar pain in my right ankle, drenched T-shirt, eyes stinging with sweat. Going home? Just going. Accept the one moment you can know and become the world. Other critters don't have to. They are the world. The remedial course is for two-leggeds only.

At midnight I lie in the meadow watching stars. The crickets pulse, about once a second, to a background trill of peeper frogs. The two belong together. "A Druidic Difference Enhances Nature now." What week, what night, did they first sound? What else have I missed? And when, for that matter, when did the Milky Way start? The crickets belong to night and the stars. Do they know the stars? Their music does.

The bear, the big bear, he's hot in the dog-day heat. He lumbers slow in the lower meadow, swaying, brown in the sun with blondish glints. I looked when I heard his feet snapping sticks. In all the Rogue River Canyon, only the bear and I are that clumsy. I sneak down by the barn for a better glimpse, but he smells or hears me, stops, stares at whatever his poor narrow eyes can discern, and takes off downhill, crashing heavily through brush. Then I hear him walking again, lumbering slow into deeper woods, where it might be cooler and there aren't any weirdos harassing him.

Last light in the tops of the pines and firs. The canyon gone to murmurous blue shadow. The country settled into itself, glad with a secret it need not speak.

Ah, the natural simplicities. A wasp alights on the clothesline, jaws and forelegs working a white moth. He devours the body headfirst, a hunched parenthesis around his prey, white wing-bits adrift in the sunny breeze. In half a minute the meal is complete, the moth's wings to earth somewhere, its body buzzing from the clothesline. The afternoon resumes. The afternoon never stopped.

Tonight the full moon rose over Rattlesnake Ridge. Through binoculars, first a white radiance, a garish backlight above the ridge. Then the top curve slid into view, silhouetting the snaggy ridgetop trees, and the old, pocked, familiar face transcended the ridge, lifting loose in the summer sky.

Latest thought on simplicity. As the poet wrote four centuries ago: *"Fool,"* *said my Muse to me, "look in thy heart, and write."*

This evening, dusk going to dark, the doe stood alone by the apple trees looking out on the meadow. She scarcely moved, not ears, not tail. An air of waiting. I wondered what she was up to, then thought: Why can't a deer be up to nothing? This August evening she might like simply to pause and look. But I also thought: Has she lost the second fawn too?

Cloudy this morning, mottled gray, no trace of blue. A cool breeze. How long since a day began this way? How pleasant it is, how various the forest greens in this subdued light, the broadleafs and needle trees. How rich the sere, towheaded meadow. There's a trace of yellow in the top boughs of the walnut trees. Fall is my season. It always feels like coming home, not knowing I'd been away.

The little squirrel's on the deck again, ripping shreds of newspaper in a cardboard box. He wads his bulging cheeks, strip after strip, paper ends crinkling from his mouth. All the news that fits. He'll have warmth and shelter from it, more than I got. He might as well have the paper in front of me, too. No news here. And I have just two more months.

September fourth and I woke to a patter of rain. A sparse rhythm, scarcely enough to settle the dust, but rain! Now, at midnight, I'm on the deck in my rocker listening to the river's hushed voice. In Virginia once, on the Blue Ridge, my mother had me lie down on dry rocks and listen with one ear. Nothing at first, then I heard it—faint, steady, the whispery rumor of water, alive below.

This afternoon, when I went to the garden, the little bear was in the meadow eating apples and leisurely shitting. What makes bears so exciting? Even this fellow, who couldn't kill me if he wanted to. They can stand on their hind legs. The claws don't always show in their people-like prints. And they do as they please. They show us our careless original selves. He grins, I swear, as he squats to defecate, then shambles cross-meadow to his woods. He'll sleep well tonight. He'll sleep well all winter.

◆

Driving in, on the gravel road nearing the homestead turnoff, I came to that open view down the canyon of Kelsey Creek, the hilled and furrowed landscape falling away toward the sinuous Rogue. Shafts of sunlight slanted down to the wooded earth through pearl and silver clouds. The West, the open West, where Time takes all the time in the world winding its way through Eternity.

◆

Simplicity? I resist. I like this language, language, phrases and images tumbling through me. I sieve some out and set it down and see if it grows. I know there's a truer knowing, simpler, deeper than words. Yet how but by words can I find it?

◆

Hot again. As I neared the river, an osprey flapped from a treetop, his voice a shrill whistle. How was the fishing? Better for him, but the river always gives something. I love to inhale its biotic aura, I love its riffles, its white and green rapids with their gray boulders, but I love most of all the slower passages, the quiet upwelling roils of its deepest pools, where the river's soul rises to the surface.

◆

The dried meadow grass is bedraggled, beaten. Deer and bear and all who have passed in the night have trod and trod and slept it down. It's a flat dun color, no color. It wants the winter. And the walnut trees, every day their green turns golder in sun.

◆

A copper-gold aura surrounds the hunter's moon tonight, a film of buttermilk clouds passing, stately, northeastward. I've been writing about my mother, her last years with Marilyn and me in Portland, and I sense her up there in the lively sky. I'll never touch her blotched and wrinkled hand again, but what we lose in love somehow returns to us in the wild beauty of this world.

Is not the bucket of apples I carry from the garden to spill for the deer and bears as important as any task of my life?

Tonight a steady soaking rain. It's lovely to turn inward, a fire in the woodstove, the heavens dancing a measured symphony on the cedar-shake roof. So I wanted to write about my mother. Why am I always the last to know?

About four this afternoon, a distant honky-tonk stirs wings in my chest. Goose music. Honk on, travelers. I thought simplicity would come with the place, but you can't slip it on like a shirt. You have to make it. "I am thinking by what long discipline and at what cost a man learns to speak simply at last."

In the pale light of late October, bright with lastnesses, wind stirred the treetops and scattered leaves all afternoon, then at sundown lulled. I didn't see the doe arrive. She stands by the apple trees, nosing the grass for fallen fruit. Her fawn is spotless and her fawn is a he, small antler knobs above his eyes. He stands apart from his mother, a young deer eligible for winter, a member of this country. Somewhere his twin is a scatter of bones, its body gone into others, but this deer watches, he tunes his ears, he sniffs the air for them both. Dusk deepens into dark, the deer fade, and veils of mist rise out of the canyon, lit by a last-quarter moon. Seven pears ripen on the windowsill. Soft hiss from the propane lamp. Papers, notebooks all over the table. I am here and far away from here. In a few days I leave for home. My pencil has opened a path that looks like a long one. I expect it to loop and branch, stutter, dead-end, turn back on itself and then forward, time and again, and time and again I will follow.

The Mother of Beauty

Is there no change of death in paradise?
Does ripe fruit never fall? Or do the boughs
Hang always heavy in that perfect sky . . .

Wallace Stevens, "Sunday Morning"

When Marilyn and I moved to Portland from California in 1988, we brought my mother from the coast of Maine to live with us. Zilla was eighty and faltering, both physically and mentally. She had a slow-developing case of Alzheimer's disease, or something that acted like Alzheimer's, as well as high blood pressure and the beginnings of congestive heart failure. She could walk, with a cane on her left side and me on her right, but one circuit around our city block was enough to wear her out for the rest of the day.

One afternoon in July of 1992, Zilla fell in the bathroom and broke her right hip. The fall may have been precipitated by a stroke, though that never was confirmed. The EMTs rushed her to the Emmanuel Hospital emergency room, where two or three doctors (we arrived just before a shift change) examined her and spoke briefly with me. My mother's hip was x-rayed, and an orthopedist showed me the expected news: The neck of her right femur had cleanly snapped. The orthopedist conferred on the phone with a colleague of my mother's personal physician—who, unluckily, was away on vacation—and learned the essentials of her chart. Most notably, he was informed that Zilla had at least one damaged heart valve from a childhood bout with rheumatic fever. The orthopedist recommended immediate surgery to repair the hip, with either a pin or a replacement. It was the only way she would have a chance of walking again, he told me, and if she didn't walk she almost certainly would die before long of pneumonia or some other infection.

My mother had been unable to speak since her fall. She was conscious, but it was far from certain that she understood in medical terms what had happened to her and what her choices were. I had to decide for her, and I agreed to the surgery. The operation went well until near the end, when my mother's heart failed. The medical team worked hard and quickly, and after an hour of touch and go they managed to get her stabilized.

In the intensive care unit, a respirator billowed my mother's lungs to a steady gasping beat through a tube inserted through her nose. She had an IV in one arm, she was catheterized for urine, she was wired to an EKG monitor through four patches on her chest, and a delicate high-tech sensor had been introduced through a vein in her shoulder into the right side of her heart and through the heart into the pulmonary artery, there to detect fluctuations in blood pressure and report the information to a monitor above the bed.

My mother's eyes were closed, her mouth open, her head tilted to one side, shifting rhythmically with the rising and falling of her ventilated chest. She looked puny among the tubes and wires and monitors, her white hair matted. She was there and she was nowhere.

Zilla was in intensive care for two days. Eventually a kind and forthright internist told us that she might stay alive indefinitely on the respirator, but only alive. If she were going to recover she would have showed signs by now. The surgery simply had overtaxed her heart, which already carried the burden of forcing blood through a calcified aortic valve. She had no resilience, no resources in reserve. At this point, the internist advised, we might want to think about taking her off the respirator.

We did just that the next day, after my brother had arrived. Zilla, tough bird that she was, went on breathing on her own. She lived another few days, out of intensive care, trammeled only by an IV to maintain her fluid balance and an oxygen cannula on her nose. She drifted for a while between sleep and semi-waking, then slept steadily and died, eight days after entering the hospital.

Every doctor and nurse who treated or attended my mother at the end of her life acted capably, responsibly, and sensitively, and I believe the same of my wife, my brother, and myself. It's a story with no culprit, no villain, yet it troubles me.

I knew some things about Zilla that the doctors and nurses didn't. I knew that she had volunteered, six months earlier at the dinner table, that she had a feeling she might not live much longer, and that she was little troubled by the prospect of death. I knew her religion's teaching—she was a late-life spiritual pilgrim—that the death of the body is not an extinction but a liberation of the real being, the soul, and I knew that her religion, despite her dementia, remained real and central to her. I knew she had meditated on her departure, worked at overcoming her fear, sought fortitude in scripture and poetry. I knew that in the four years she lived with us she had more than once expressed an explicit wish to die, though at other times she had shown a fear of death. I knew that Zilla had been a lively and fiercely independent woman, and that the humiliating infirmities of age sat not at all well with her.

I knew these things, yet almost automatically I chose surgery. The orthopedist had put it bluntly. She wouldn't walk again without surgery, and if she didn't walk she would die. I wish, now, that I had asked the doctor to assess Zilla's *chances* of walking again after the surgery, given her age and frail condition and the possibility that she had been felled by a stroke. And though I understood, of course, that any surgery posed a risk, no one specifically discussed with me—I did not ask anyone to discuss with me—the degree of risk to the particular patient in question, a failing eighty-four-year-old with a damaged heart. I know the risk could not have been pinned down in numbers, but we should have talked about it. I let the orthopedist and the intense energy of the emergency room make the decision for me. My own shocked panic said, *Yes, do everything. Please do it now.*

If I had chosen against surgery, I would have spared my mother the stress of a major operation and an awful travail in intensive care. I would have spared her the misery of a ventilator opening and closing her lungs like a big fist in her chest. To have declined the operation would have consigned her to death, but now I ask myself what I wish I had asked at the time: Once she had fallen, once she had broken her hip and possibly suffered a stroke, wasn't she, barring a miracle, consigned to death in any case? Wasn't death thoroughly written in her situation, there to be read by anyone with eyes to see? Wasn't the little room of hope we huddled in, doctors and family alike, actually a room of denial?

At the time, of course, that room seems the only place to be. Outside, the weather is terrible, impossible. The technical expertise exercised while you wait in the room seems unquestionably right. Everyone wants only the best, everyone wants life. But were we—doctors, family, all of us— were we really serving my mother's life, my mother's being, by conspiring to prolong a physical existence that had arrived at its final passage?

Another question I didn't ask at the time, didn't come close to asking, and would have found it intensely uncomfortable to ask: If death by pneumonia is the likely outcome without surgery, what is that death like? I know now that it tends to be, with oxygen and morphine, relatively comfortable—a slow depression of all systems, a coma, and the end. (Sir William Osler, the father of internal medicine, called pneumonia "the old man's friend.") My wife and brother and I, and other relatives and friends, would have stood a better chance of communicating with Zilla if she had not gone into surgery. Maybe we could have brought her home. Even if she hadn't been able to speak, she might have been able to express herself through hand squeezes, through smiles and tears. Or maybe not, but in any event, we would have had more time with her before she slipped into a coma, time for the affirmations and regrets and the simple need to be together that the dying of a loved one evokes in us. And *her* time, her last time on Earth, would have been far less troubled.

In an earlier era — the nineteenth century, certainly, and the first decades of the twentieth — things probably would have gone as I've just described. Those around my mother, and my mother too if she was able, would have recognized that death was near, and death would have proceeded by its own course in its own time. When it arrived, we might have washed her body, dressed her as she loved to dress, held a wake for her. As was common in the late 1800s, we might have taken a photograph of her as she lay on her bed — her accomplished body, her completed physical being, frail and in pain no longer.

Please understand, it is not at all my wish to repudiate our present medical knowledge and technical capacities, even if that were possible. My mother lived a long and active life; a hundred or two hundred years ago, her life might have been as active but it wouldn't have been as long. I do think, though, that in forestalling death as we have done, in extending the human life span through the application of the medical profession's technical genius, we have incurred losses along with our gains, and that we will face further losses with further gains. I'll tell another story, a briefer one.

A friend in England, a former Jain monk named Satish Kumar, once spoke in an interview about the death of his mother in India. When she was eighty or so she said to her family, "I'm now too old. I can't cook, I can't see, I can't do anything for you. What point is there in carrying on? From tomorrow, I'm going to start dying." She made the rounds of her village, stopping in to visit relatives, friends, everyone she knew. "I have come to say goodbye, because I am going to die," she told them. Then she began to fast. As she lay peacefully, bearing herself into death, the villagers chanted, sang hymns, prayed and meditated around her. They did their part to launch her on the voyage she had chosen.

Satish's mother had reached a limit, acknowledged what that limit asked of her, and made a decision. It could be said that she committed suicide, but her act was of such clarity and integrity and gentleness that it bears no resemblance to suicide as we ordinarily understand it, as an anguished act of violence against oneself, an act that inevitably works further anguish on the suicide's family and friends. We use the phrase "to take one's life." Satish's mother did nothing so abrupt or destructive. She *completed* her life; she did not take but gave it. She was an apple on a tree, ripe and growing overripe. One day soon — a good day, like all others — the apple would surely drop from the branch. Satish's mother affirmed, by choice, the most natural of events.

My mother was more ambivalent about dying than Satish's was, and both her Alzheimer's and her stoic New England character made it difficult for her to express personal wishes, but she had given what I now see as clear signs that she was ready to go. When she told me, six months before she fell, that she might not live much longer, I asked how she felt about that. Without hesitation Zilla said, "Thankful for everything I've had. It's been a privilege."

I wish I could have accepted what my mother was telling me. I wish I had tried harder to draw out her thoughts and feelings in the weeks that followed. Instead of merely going on with the usual care I gave her, the daily humdrum, I could have helped her imagine how she wanted to meet her death. I could have read to her from her religious books, meditated with her, played her tapes of sacred music if she wanted to hear them. I could have asked her if she would like to fast. I could have notified everyone she might want to see before she died.

I could have acknowledged and made an honorable place in our household for the guest soon to arrive, who had traveled eighty-four years to meet my mother. If I had helped her welcome him, helped her greet and begin to know him, perhaps he wouldn't have had to trip her in the bathroom to accomplish what he had come to do. Or perhaps she wouldn't have had to trip herself. We're not certain that my mother was felled by a stroke, or — as sometimes happens — by a spontaneous break in her fragile hip. It's possible that she felled herself. Caring for her had put me and my marriage under a lot of stress, and my mother knew it. Tending to her things in the weeks after she died, I found two items in her deer-hide purse. One was her pendulum, of the kind dowsers use, which she had sometimes consulted to help her make decisions. The other was a slip of paper from a fortune cookie. It read, "Leave your boat and travel on firm ground."

I didn't make a place for death because I didn't want my mother to die. That came of my love for her, but it was also a selfishness: I didn't want to feel what I knew I would have to feel if she did die. I didn't want to be burdened with my mother's death, and in stonewalling against it I was acting out the deep denial of death that pervades our culture. Death is taboo, a hush-hush deal, an unseemly rumor that might turn out not to be true, we seem to hope, if we ignore it long enough. Dying is a little like sex—everyone does it, but no one, in polite society, talks about it.

After all, who dies in the modern world? Certainly not us. Our birthdays conspire to prove that we get older, but we counter that sinister trend by devotedly making ourselves younger. We dye our hair, plump out wrinkles, sweat off fat, tone our muscles, improve our diets, curb our vices, replace our joints, have great sex longer, and stay actively engaged in our work and hobbies and recreations. We can't possibly die—we're too busy. Only others are subject to death, those unfortunates who didn't care for themselves correctly, who didn't improve their lot if poor, who indulged themselves if rich, who didn't see the doctor when they should have, whose self-esteem was too low or anger too high, who didn't laugh or meditate or play enough golf, who didn't see to their personal growth as they should have, who drove cars too fast or themselves too hard, who took too much whiskey or not enough garlic and omega-3s, who should have drunk ten glasses of water each day, whether or not they were thirsty, and preserved themselves through psychotherapy or high colonics or deep massage.

But we do age, despite ourselves, and when death draws nigh and will no longer be ignored, we do not go gently into that good night. We hold out with everything we have. We go down fighting. Look at the phrases we read every day in the newspaper, and hear on radio and TV, and sometimes find issuing from our own mouths: *She fought bravely for life. He lost his long battle with leukemia. She was cut down by a stroke. We are making progress in the war on cancer.* This is the language of mortal combat, in which the practitioners and recipients of medicine heroically struggle together against death, and in a certain limited sense we are winning the struggle. We the people demand longer life, medical science provides it, and we the people take for granted each incremental boon and demand still longer life. Where will it end, this war? Will we be satisfied when the average life span reaches ninety years? A hundred and ten? Or will we settle for nothing less than genetically tinkering ourselves into immortality?

The financial costs of the war on death are immense and growing. The bill for the final eight days of my mother's life came to well over thirty thousand dollars. She had no resources, and we in the family couldn't pay it either. Medicare and Medicaid paid it, or paid part of it, which is to say that the American people paid it. And thirty thousand, I feel sure, is a cheaper tab than many others incur who spend their last days or weeks or months in the hospital undergoing intensive and expensive treatment. Heroic interventions command heroic fees. The cost of health care insurance already ranges from formidable to staggering for many of those who can afford it, and over forty million Americans can't.

If government health-care entitlements founder in the next few decades, as many expect, even as life-prolonging techniques and technology grow ever costlier, will long life become an amenity reserved for the wealthy? What will it mean to a people who respect the principle, at least, that all persons are created equal, if winning the war against death proves a victory for only an elite few? Probably the fairest approach would be to cut expenses by rationing end-of-life care in order to provide at least basic medical care for everyone, including those who don't now have it except through the emergency room. Such rationing, as in the British system, would likely have meant no hip replacement for my mother. I might have railed about that at the time, but now I think it might have produced a better outcome — for my mother, for our family, and for the American people.

But it's not the financial costs that concern me most. Americans are dying miserable, arduous deaths, in many cases far more protracted than my mother's, because of the warfare mentality of modern medicine. We are dying more closely embraced by tubes and wires and chemicals than by family and friends. And we are dying in this way often with no legitimate hope of winning anything more than a brief extension, usually deeply troubled, of a life that has come to its close. Living to the end and past the end has acquired the force of a strict duty, an orthodoxy, for all concerned. Even when the pained and anguished patient is ready to leave the boat, too often she feels she cannot do so without the permission, stated or implicit, of the loved ones who rally around her, and the pained and anguished loved ones themselves too often fear that to grant such permission amounts to betrayal. And so the boat rocks offshore in rough waters, the weather awful, no one at peace, all hands rowing as hard as they can against the waves that soon will beach the boat in any case despite their mightiest efforts.

But it is one thing to speak of the elderly dying, quite another to speak of the young. The loss of a mother in her eighties is a sadness, but she, at least, has completed the arc of a lifetime. The death of a child, a teenager, a young adult, seems a gratuitous cruelty, an injustice, a tragedy. Here the metaphor of warfare seems more justified. We want the youthful patient and all around her to pursue even the most minute possibility of recovery, to fight come hell or high water for the decades of living that ought to have been her birthright.

Here's a third story, and this is a harder one. A daughter of good friends of ours was diagnosed at age thirteen with non-Hodgkins lymphoma. She received the best treatment available, at Stanford Medical Center, and went into remission. Five years passed, and Susie and her family dared to breathe again. Half a decade means, often, that one has beaten the cancer. But in the sixth year, when Susie was nineteen, it came back. A blood stem cell transplant and radiation didn't work. Susie, now twenty, didn't want to go through the ravages of chemotherapy again. Her focus turned to alternative treatments as she, her boyfriend, and her family cast about for hope. Their research turned up a doctor in Chicago who was trying, with some success, a combination of diet and alternative healing modalities together with limited chemotherapy. The doctor was reputable, his credentials fine.

Susie was sick, coughing a lot, feeling miserable. Some urged her to try the new treatment. Some were uncertain. Susie told her boyfriend that she feared she would die in Chicago. She told one friend—but not her family—that she didn't want to go, that one of her doctors had recommended hospice rather than another hospital, and that she had been thinking about her funeral. Susie wavered, but in the end, she and her boyfriend flew to Chicago to begin the experimental treatment.

Very quickly she developed pneumonia. Her family and several close friends came to Chicago to be with her. Susie was tubed and wired, her condition grave. More equipment was wheeled in. Fluids were pumped into her body. Susie's heartbeat went flat. Everyone around her was possessed by an agonized desire to keep a brave and beautiful young woman alive. They fought her death as hard as they could, and that is how Susie died—surrounded by loved ones but very much in battle, two thousand miles from home, her departure from the world overrun by machines and techniques attacking the illness that had overrun her body. In the war on death, the battlefield is the body.

In retrospect, that most privileged of perspectives, hospice might have been a wiser choice. But Susie wanted to live, and everyone who knew her wanted her to live. She chose to try one more treatment, and why wouldn't she? Relatively new therapies had extended her life by seven years, allowing her a taste, at least, of adulthood. One of my best friends, a fiction writer, is alive today because recently evolved techniques and medicines have beaten his acute lymphocytic leukemia into remission. Had he been stricken a few years earlier, his wife would probably be a widow, his two young sons fatherless, his friends and family bereft. If I should fall gravely ill, I would probably choose as Susie and my writer friend chose; I would hope to live, I would ask medical science to do everything in its power.

But what is reasonable hope, and what is the hope of Tantalus, who perpetually reaches for fruit too high to grasp? Each new cure or treatment raises expectations of further advances, but medicines and procedures at any level can never be entirely effective, and not every disease can be outright banished from nature. Cancer patients are living longer these days, but in most cases the difference amounts to a few added months spent in sickness from the disease and its treatment. If we ever achieve an environmentally sane society we might reduce the incidence of cancer, but cancer will still occur, and so will other afflictions. Tuberculosis, once thought to have been virtually extincted, has returned to become the number-one infectious cause of adult death in the world. Any year now, any decade, a new form of flu virus could recapitulate or far transcend the deadly pandemic of 1918. Antibiotics were supposed to permanently subdue all dangerous microbes; now, microbes are demonstrating natural selection so quickly and clearly that even creationists should be able to get it. And diseases previously unknown, such as AIDS and the West Nile virus, arise and spread rapidly in our humanly engrossed world.

In short, our efforts to control and prevent diseases — not to mention accidents — will always have limits, and that means we will never be able to save every child or young man or young woman, let alone every eighty-four-year-old mother who falls in the bathroom. And so, even as medicine works hard to save those it can, shouldn't we on both sides of the medical relationship learn to make an intelligent peace with death, when it will not be denied, instead of fighting it to the bitter end? Wouldn't it enlarge our humanity to recover, from beneath the heavy overlays of technological optimism and military rhetoric, the ability to discern and respect the arrival of death in a human life? Wouldn't it ennoble life to honor its natural end? Susie in her twenty years lived a beautiful life, as did my mother in her eighty-four. I wish both had died a beautiful death.

Marilyn's step-grandfather, Harry, died at either 103 or 106, depending on which records you consult. (He lied about his age to get into the Navy and sailed with Teddy Roosevelt's White Fleet.) He suffered some of the lesser infirmities of age but nothing debilitating, nothing that made him physically miserable. He lived in a pleasant Seattle retirement home with a view of the water. He was well attended, visited regularly by Marilyn's father and stepmother. He was not depressed in the medical sense. Yet Harry prayed every day, in his last years, for Jesus to come and take him. He wondered why he was still alive. His predicament reminded me of the epochally old French woman who died around the time that he did. I think she was 121. She was quoted near the end as saying, "I feel as though God has forgotten me."

The wish of the old for release from life echoes in the oldest stories of our civilization. Aurora, goddess of the dawn, who was in love with Tithonus, a mortal, petitioned Zeus to make Tithonus live forever, as she would. This Zeus did, but Aurora, in her excitement, had forgotten to ask that he exempt her lover from aging. And so Tithonus grew old and decrepit. Shrunken, in pain, hardly able to move, he begged for death, but death would not oblige him. At last Aurora shut him in a room where he babbled maniacally, his mind as ruined as his body. By one account he shriveled and jabbered to such a degree that Aurora turned him into a small, bony, and seasonally loud creature that we call the grasshopper.

Researchers now investigating the genetic basis of the human life span, with the hope of doing some tinkering, ought to consult the story of Tithonus before they tinker much more. And they also should consult the many stories in the Western tradition about human hubris, or overreaching arrogance. Some of the laws relevant to our existence are not of the scientific kind. One of them, well known to the ancients but not to us, is that the gods hate hubris, and that its consequences usually are grim.

I don't underestimate the tinkerers. They are technical wonder-workers. But even if they find a way to extend the human life span *and* to retard or deactivate the aging process, I think their bioengineering wizardry will prove an ill gift. In his poem "Sunday Morning," the American modernist Wallace Stevens wrote, "Death is the mother of beauty," the only repeated phrase in the poem. He meant, I believe, that it is only because of mortality, and our awareness of it, that we can perceive and value the beautiful. It is only because of mortality that beauty can exist, and that we humans can love the beautiful in each other and our surroundings.

In a life without death and knowledge of death, what could stir our passions? Without the need to realize ourselves before we die, to cross the mountains or sail the sea, what would become of our topography of essential desires and emotions, what variation from the flat plain of paradisal bliss? What would drive us to write poems or symphonies that amounted to more than repetitive celebrations of the unchanging boughs that Stevens imagined, hanging heavy in a perfect sky with ripe fruit that never falls? Why would we tell or listen to stories? How *could* we, because in that paradise, without desire and hope and fear, there would be no stories, no beginnings and no endings, no past and no future — only a single, eternal, enslaving moment beneath those boughs of fruit whose very sweetness would be dulled, if we could taste it at all, by the easeful death of our indefinitely ongoing lives.

Like any true privilege, conscious being is both a boon and a burden. It is, in Wendell Berry's phrase, "a mighty blessing we cannot bear for long." We simply are not made, in body or in psyche, to carry the burden of life indefinitely, just as we are not made to stay permanently awake. Sleep rests the body, but even more so, by regular immersion in the soothing waters of oblivion, it rests the mind and spirit. With sleep we are eligible for happiness. Without it we go crazy. Without it we can't live, and I have a strange hunch that we could not live without death, either. Death is the warrant that we are truly alive, that we have truly been here at all. It is the non-negotiable price of our unlikely incorporation as living beings, members of a universe in which all creatures born, from bacteria to blue whales, must perish too. New lives are ever coming into the world, and they can grow only from the compost of those that have died. *We* grow from the compost of those that have died, and others will grow from the compost of our own accomplished lives.

From sleep, of course, we expect to wake. From death we don't know what to expect. It is a mystery, *the* mystery, momentous and ill-defined, about which all of us are poorly informed. Is it the end of the story of "I," the living individual, or is it the beginning of a new chapter, or a new book? Is it an extinction? A passageway? A judgment? A joy? We all have hopes and fears and intimations. Those who seem to feel most certain—spiritual fundamentalists who find the tangible world unreal, material fundamentalists who find everything *but* the tangible world unreal—are the ones I trust least. I trust Henry James, who carried into his deathbed his resolve "to be one of the people on whom nothing is lost." He said, in his last days: "So it has come at last—the Distinguished Thing." And I trust Henry David Thoreau, who, as he lay dying of consumption, was pressed by a friend to tell what he could see through the doorway opening before him. "One world at a time," Thoreau replied.

We think of sunrise as a beginning and sunset as an ending, but each is equally a beginning and an end. Their colors are close kin, and those colors interfuse to form the daylight by which we see our way and know ourselves, in which we bloom for a time in bones and flesh and blood, in which we touch fingers to skin and look into the eyes of others as they look into ours, in which we love and sing and weep and suffer and live. The light that fades in an old man's eyes as he sinks into death is the same light that burns in a young woman's eyes as she gives birth to her child.

The human species, as it developed self-consciousness, developed an awareness of death, and those ancestors of ours grappled with its mystery pretty much as we do today—the best they could. Neanderthals, fifty thousand years ago, gave flints and axes and medicinal flowers to the graves of their dead; I would guess that they also keened and chanted, wept, perhaps sang. In North America, Paleo-Indians and their descendants, like all human cultures, spun stories about death. Those that I know best—in *Coyote Was Going There*, Jarold Ramsey's inestimable anthology of Native American stories from the Oregon Country—recapitulate archetypal themes that we Euro-Americans know from our own tradition, in particular the stories of Orpheus and Pandora.

In a tale of the Wishram, a Columbia River people, Coyote and Eagle go to the land of the dead to find and retrieve their wives and families, who have recently died. Eagle, the elder, knows the way; he instructs Coyote. In the great underground chamber of departed spirits, they first must kill Frog Woman—a bad sign, surely, for pilgrims intent on reversing the finality of death—whose practice it is to swallow the moon every evening and disgorge it at morning. (In the land of the dead, everything works oppositely to the way of things among the living.) Coyote takes Frog Woman's place, choking on the moon and barely pulling off the ruse, and Eagle places in the doorway of the chamber a box he has fashioned, filled with leaves from every kind of tree and blades from every kind of grass. At daylight the dead file out of the chamber, as is their custom, and unknowingly into the box. Eagle triumphantly closes the box, tosses the moon into the sky—where it would stay—and he and Coyote set out homeward, the box humming with a sound like a great swarm of flies.

Eagle carries the box. On the third night Coyote hears voices. On the fourth night he realizes the voices are coming from the box. He presses his ear to it and makes out the voice of his wife. He smiles, he laughs with happiness. At the end of the fifth night, only a day from home, Coyote insists on carrying the box, appealing to Eagle's vanity—how will it look, he says, arriving among our people, if the chief is seen carrying the load? Eagle, against his better judgment, relents. Coyote takes up the box, and every time he hears the voice of his wife, he laughs. He deliberately falls behind, stops, and cracks open the box. The dead rush out in a wind that knocks Coyote to the ground. Eagle turns, sees the cloud of the dead foun-taining skyward, and goes back. Only one of the dead remains, a cripple; Eagle throws him aloft and the cripple ascends out of sight.

"Do you see what you have done?" says Eagle. "If we had brought these dead all the way back, people would not die forever, but only for a season, like these plants, whose leaves we have brought. Hereafter trees and grasses will die only in the winter, but in the spring will be green again. So it would have been with the people."

"We can go back and catch them again," Coyote blurts.

But Eagle knows better. "We would not know how to find them," he says. "They are now where the moon is, up in the sky."

So the story ends, with classic rough news: What we do, we do once only. And why do we die? Because we smile and laugh when we hear our wife's or husband's voice. Because we are impatient and cannot wait. Because we are vain and foolish. Because we live and because we love. Because we are born into beauty and yearn to become that beauty, even as we cradle the small candle of the self by which we know it.

Marilyn's mother died six years after mine, four months after her cancer had been diagnosed. Half a year before the diagnosis, when we were visiting, Winona seemed to be feeling fine but evidently had felt an inkling. "Don't you kids worry if something happens to me," she told us, out of the blue. "I've had a good life." The cancer was inoperable, it turned out, but the doc-tors told her that radiation might buy her more time. Winona declined the discomfort and indignity of that. She lived right on into her death, ambu-latory at first, then bed-bound, taking medication as the pain intensified.

Marilyn moved to her mother's home in Leavenworth, Washington, and attended her (with the vital support of hospice), doing everything from fluffing pillows to turning her mother in bed to administering pain-killing anal suppositories. When I was with them, I saw something won-derful happen. Winona had not been a particularly warm or nurturing mother. I think it does her no injustice to say that her gifts were more physical than emotional or intellectual. She was a sportswoman, a perennial golf champion at her club who outplayed women twenty years her junior. Toward Marilyn she had been pushy, sometimes overbearing. She had more than once made comments that cut to the quick.

As she neared death, however, Winona warmed. She wanted to be touched, to hold hands. She spoke affectionately to her daughter, expressed her love and gratefulness. She laughed readily. Her arriving death brought with it that final gift for the two of them, a gift that could have presented itself and been received in no other way. And to Winona's broad face, her dark hair damp with sweat, it brought a nobility I hadn't seen in her. The sportswoman was a brave soul, her courage surely signed in her candid, clear-spirited beauty. That January, in her last weeks, she often verged into fantasy. She thought she was booked on a cruise, was worried about finding her purse. She had some traveling to do. Eventually she slipped into several days of steady sleep, and very early one morning—a good morning, like all others—her breathing came to an undramatic halt.

"I think she's gone," Marilyn whispered, more awe in her voice than sorrow. I rose from the easy chair where I had been sleeping, and silently, for a long time, we watched. Outside the window in the frigid morning, drifted snow took on the pink and golden hues of sunrise, and a chickadee came and went from the feeder, picking one sunflower seed at a time.

A WORD IN FAVOR OF ROOTEDNESS

On the afternoon of February 7, 2002, Marilyn was in Portland, a hundred and twenty miles north, and I was doing some errands closer to home in Eugene. One of my missions was to buy the second edition of *The Norton Book of Nature Writing*, which had just been published. A short distance away in the bookstore parking lot, as I got out of the truck, a big Douglas fir limb broke from its trunk and hit the pavement next to an espresso drive-through, bouncing once before settling. This was the first I knew that a strenuous wind was blowing. I went into the store to buy the book, and when I came out a limb had fallen from another tree and wind was surging. The drive-through barista had called it a day. As I drove off I switched the radio on and learned that a major windstorm had hit the area. Had hit. We do pick up on current events, we humans, but at our own special-needs pace. Every bird and squirrel in Lane County had been dealing with the wind as I'd been driving to town and scanning the bookstore shelves in the Nature section for the object of my interest.

I started for home — twenty-some miles west of Eugene — right away. The radio told me that Highway 126 west, the direct route, was cut off by downed trees, so I shot north on Interstate 5, the roundabout route. I exited west through Harrisburg, waited on Highway 99 south — in darkness now — as a crew of hardworking householders chainsawed through a big conifer that had fallen across the roadway and rolled sections of trunk off into the ditch. I headed on, dreading what I'd find. Our house sits in a grove of Douglas firs, ranging from pecker-poles to middling adolescents to hundred-and-forty-foot veterans three-and-a-half feet through, and the biggest stand within thirty feet of the house. Every time the wind kicks up, small branches hit the roof with loud knocks or thumps. When we bought the place, in 1994, half the roof had just been replaced after major windfall damage. During our eight years in the house we had on several occasions watched the trees swaying more than we liked in a major gale. We said spells for the grip of roots and the flexibility of fiber.

On Territorial Road and then Butler Road, nearing home, I drove the truck slowly over a cushiony bed of broken-off fir boughs, veering around small trees and large limbs. Twice I had to get out and strain to swing a downed pecker-pole far enough that the truck could get by. As I turned right on Sheffler Road, one mile from home, I was hoping it wouldn't rain, because I didn't have enough tarps to cover a caved-in roof. Let it be just one tree, I bargained with whoever might be listening. I took the familiar left turn into our driveway and the headlights swung onto the house — its roof festooned with fir boughs, but all the trees still standing, limbs stirring languidly in what was left of the great February windstorm. A couple of hefty branches had fallen, injuring nothing more than rhododendrons and one pancaked fern.

The power was out, of course — it wouldn't come back for three days — and so I lit candles, built a fire in the woodstove, poured a stout whiskey, lifted the glass to all Great Spirits, those in the air, those in the glass, and those of other habitats, and settled into a soft chair to wait for Marilyn, feeling very happy about where I lived.

In 1966, eighteen years old, I navigated a blue-and-white Jeep with a bad electrical system up U.S. 101 from San Francisco, having left my mother's home in Washington, D.C., two weeks earlier. I hit the Oregon border around 1:00 AM on a very foggy night in late summer and pulled into a wayside north of Brookings. I parked the Jeep on a downslope, stumbled toward the beach in the thick dark, sat on a rock, and let the boom and wash and shrill withdrawing hiss of breakers soothe my overheated head. After a while I went down to touch the Pacific Ocean for the first time and got my sneakers wet. In the morning the Jeep started without a rolling jump, which I took to be a sign.

I was on my way to Reed College, in Portland, where I would try to be a student and would succeed for a year and a half. My relations with my new natural surroundings turned out to be far more pleasurable than my relations with books and classrooms and the anxieties of late adolescence. One stormy night in the fall of my freshman year, not far outside my room in the Old Dorm Block, a shot of lightning exploded the top of one of the tallest trees on campus, a solitary Douglas fir, and turned it into a flaming torch. I wasn't lucky enough to see the strike, but I did come along in time to behold a crazy spectacle — yellow flames blazing a hundred feet overhead in the top of a wet dark tree. Another sign. "This," I said to myself, "is a cool place."

My enthusiasm waxed further a year later when a ripping windstorm blew in off the Pacific. On campus, with friends, I watched trees snapping and tumbling on the other side of the Willamette River in southwest Portland, taking down power lines and popping a transformer now and then with a hail of sparks. We hollered and cheered, being far better situated (as I would learn) than Lewis and Clark and their men had been in December 1805, when, newly arrived near the mouth of the Columbia, mildewed, all paddled-out, living on spoiling salmon loaf bought from upriver Indians, they were assaulted by a similar storm. "The winds violent," wrote William Clark in his journal. "Trees falling in every derection, whorl winds, with gusts of rain Hail & Thunder, this kind of weather lasted all day. Certainly one of the worst days that ever was!" A rough welcome to the Oregon Country — and *then* the long, gray, sopping winter, sleepless from flea bites, eating what little they could find to shoot, their whiskey long exhausted.

It was Oregon, wild and lovely and violent Oregon, that ruined my academic career. How could I keep my nose in Herodotus, my ears in windy seminars, my spirit in dolorous, fluorescent classrooms, while outside swarmed a green paradise of mountains and rivers and seacoast and forests of gargantuan trees? And so I ditched Reed and took up backpacking and mountain climbing. I hiked the Hoh River Trail in Olympic National Park, from the mossy rainforest of colossal cedars where it begins up to brilliant alpine meadows and Mount Olympus, and later I trekked a few sections of the Pacific Crest Trail in the Oregon Cascades. On Mount Hood, my first big climb, I couldn't believe my Eastern eyes. I was standing eleven thousand feet in the air atop a snowbound volcano with nothing around me but everything, an oceanic vista such as I had never seen or imagined, the wavy verdant landscape with its roads and towns and other human marks — trifles from that vantage, chicken scratches — stretching vastly in every direction, the Cascades punctuated with snowy exclamations as far as I could see. Mount St. Helens (then still a perfect cone, the Fujiyama of the Cascades), Mount Adams, and Mount Rainier stood to the north, and Jefferson, Three-fingered Jack, Washington, and the Three Sisters to the south.

To put shekels in my pocket I went to work for a while as a logger in southern Washington State, under Mount St. Helens, my youthful enthusiasm dissolving any sense of contradiction between loving the trees of paradise and leveling them. High-lead logging has some of the brutish appeal of terrible weather. An entire mountainside of trees has been clear-cut, some of them huge old-growth cedars and hemlocks, and bucked into thirty- and forty-foot lengths. A hundred-foot steel tower is set up on a punched-in road, a gargantuan network of cables is strung down the hillside, and workers like me, again and again, scramble to noose cables around logs and clear the hell out of the way as several tons of ex-trees at a time go up the hill under protest, scattering other logs and uprooting stumps and gouging furrows in the muddy earth. It's exhausting work. The chance to witness spectacular violence is about all that saves it.

I left the Northwest a couple of times to pursue my personal confusions in San Francisco, which seemed a necessary thing to do in the late '60s and early '70s, but I kept coming back. I never considered living in the East again. I didn't know much for sure in my early twenties, but I knew I had corrected the mistake of having been born and raised on the wrong coast. In 1973 I left the Bay Area for a railroad job in a part of Oregon I hadn't seen, the Klamath Basin, just east of the Cascades and north of the California line. Once again I couldn't believe my eyes. Surely this was Nevada, not Oregon. Where was the forest? Where were the merry streams, the emerald meadows? Seven years after first setting foot in the state, it was just then dawning on me that two-thirds of Oregon is semi-arid steppe and outright desert. "Won't stay long here," I said to myself.

I stayed ten years. Bleakness turned to beauty before my eyes. I grew to love the spacious distances of rimrocks and alkali lakes and junipered hills, of mountains blue on a far-off horizon. I gradually discovered the lofty pronghorn pastures of Hart Mountain, the Malheur Refuge with its seasonal bonanzas of waterfowl, the singular standing wave of Steens Mountain, the painted hills and tilted vistas of the John Day country, the psychedelic geology of Leslie Gulch, and, far to the northeast, the exuberant granitic Wallowas, nothing like the Cascades, more like a branch of the Rocky Mountains that got lost and wandered west into Oregon.

Nature, I learned over the years, has a lot on her mind in this state, a slew of wildly various thoughts, and she's committed to all of them. Forget the interior, consider the corners alone. The steep slopes of the Klamath Mountains in the southwest, where the Rogue and Illinois Rivers flow, host one of the most diverse temperate forests in the world, a green hodgepodge of broadleafs and needle trees of all forms and sizes. There are spots on the coast down there where palm trees grow. Jump four hundred miles straight east, to the Owyhee Uplands we share with Idaho and Nevada, and you can walk the lonesome sagebrush tableland all day long without sighting a single trunk, but for an occasional willow or cottonwood down in the winding canyons etched into the basalt bedrock. The Owyhees might get eight inches of moisture a year. Zag diagonally coastward to the Clatsop Plain in the northwest corner, where Lewis and Clark and their Corps of Discovery spent their triumphant and miserable winter, and you'll get a hundred and twenty inches, up to two hundred in the ferned and mossy Coast Range not far south. From that country of rainforest, of storm surf hammering the stacks and headlands, vault due eastward to a still different kind of grandeur at a place called Hat Point, beyond the Wallowas, where you'll gaze down almost six thousand feet into a vast, terraced, grassy-benched vessel of quiet called Hells Canyon. Tiny within its inner chasm, the green Snake River hurls itself through Rush Creek Rapids, its thunderous roil refined at your elevation to virtual soundlessness, a whisper of wind.

Of all the states, only California can credibly claim greater variety of landscape and extremes of climate, and California cheats by being so big. I was lured into its bosom again in the 1980s, tracking the dubious scent of a writing career, but when I came north again I came to stay. First in Portland, that good gray city of bridges and bookstores and the best beer in America, and now, for the last fifteen years, on an acre of land tucked up in the Coast Range foothills at the southern end of the Willamette Valley, the New Eden that enticed caravans of settlers over the Oregon Trail in the 1840s and '50s. Those settlers learned that the New Eden is a tad wetter than the old one, particularly down our way. The ground crawls with slugs and newts, the dank soil ridden with moles, voles, and other vermin. Our yard is more moss than grass. Marilyn and I trudge through the rains and mists in rubber boots, leaving footprints inches deep. The days are gray and gray and gray again, for month upon month. The trees drip. The mossy roof drips. The downspouts gurgle incessantly. Don't consider settling here. This is habitat for borderline lunatics.

All that keeps us going is our faith, long tested, that eventually the sun will goof up and blunder back into our sky. When trillium rise in late March and open their perfect three-pointed blooms in April, things start looking up. Pretty soon sword ferns unfurl new fronds, pale new growth appears on the tips of Douglas fir boughs, and the grass and weeds start growing an inch a day. Irritable hummingbirds buzz the kitchen windows demanding their feeder, dogwoods spread creamy rumors in the woods, blue camas hazes the bright green pastures, we hear a tentative stir from the bee tree, and the Vaux's swifts announce by a whirring of wings in the chimney that they have returned to raise a brood again on our premises. By then it's warm enough that we don't need a fire, and we decide to stay another year.

If you're going to live among large trees, it's a good idea to live among many. We've got about fifty Douglas firs on our acre, which is two-thirds wooded. (The open portion is a seasonal stream course we call Winter Creek, and we've taken to calling the whole place by the same name.) Our neighbor Allen has probably triple our tree population. He's in the same woods to the southwest of us, the property line marked by a wire fence crushed under decades of blackberry canes. Altogether, the woods is a triangular patch of three or four acres, the remnant of a larger Douglas fir forest and white oak woodland long since cleared for agriculture on the flatter land around us — Allen's organically farmed fields to the south and west, a little cattle ranch to the east. It's from the southwest that winter storms arrive, swirling up counterclockwise out of the Pacific, about forty miles away as the raven flies. The trees buffer the wind for one another, swaying in unison, sharing the burden. Their roots intertwine, too, compensating for their shallowness by working together in the softened wet soil of winter.

Our ocean was named by Ferdinand Magellan, rounding Cape Horn and dreaming westward one remarkably calm day in November 1519. The so-called Pacific can be a deadly cauldron in winter. It takes the lives of commercial fishermen every year off California and the Northwest coast, more here than in the waters of Alaska. Inland, any tree or stand of trees can be thrown by a big enough wind. The Columbus Day storm of 1962 leveled thousands of forest acres in western Oregon, and lesser wind storms and ice storms have done considerable leveling of their own. The practice of pocking a forest with small clearcuts, a staple of late-twentieth-century forestry on public lands, has contributed to the damage. Trees fare better where they stand in numbers. My father, who was a labor organizer, would have appreciated that. In the words of "Solidarity Forever," the anthem of the American labor movement, *What force on earth is weaker than the feeble strength of one, but the Union makes us strong. . . .*

From the very first, our trees taught me to tilt back my head, as I do in a cathedral. And to listen, when the wind is stirring in one of its milder moods, to its spirited play in the high crowns. Douglas fir limbs angle mildly downward from the trunk and then curve upward again as they branch out and narrow toward the tip, producing even arcs pretty consistent in degree from limb to limb. A mature tree's crown is a candelabra of many such limbs, and I can't help but sense a jauntiness in their upturned habit. It's as though the long gesture of seed says something happy, as though it rises from the ground in exuberant praise. I know what Aldo Leopold meant when he wrote, in *A Sand County Almanac*, that walking among his Wisconsin pines always gave him a curious transfusion of courage.

A few years into our stint here I decided to get to know our trees on closer terms. Harking back to my rock climbing days, I got out my old gear, bought some new, and took to exploring the vertical dimension of our acre. Not with climbing spurs — that's a young man's game, and the spurs can injure trees — but in the newer recreational style.

You begin, for a few minutes or all afternoon, depending on your luck and skill, by slinging a weighted line over a substantial lower limb, and lowering the weight — a pouch of birdshot — to the ground. Removing the pouch, you tie the line to one end of your climbing rope and pull the rope over the limb in place of the line. You then secure one end of the rope — the rough-barked trunk of the tree itself makes a handy anchor — and clip yourself into the over-the-limb length with metal ascenders, which are designed to slide easily upward on the rope but to bite immovably upon downward pressure. You lift your legs and raise the left ascender, which is clipped to sling stirrups for your boots, and then the right ascender, which is clipped to your body harness, coming to an upright stance as you do. In this way, raising first your feet and then the standing length of your body, you climb the rope. It's not the most elegant progression — you look like a fellow who can't decide whether he wants to squat or stand — but it does get you up the tree. When you reach the limb over which the rope is suspended, you hang directly from the limb and sling the line, which you have thoughtfully brought with you, over a higher limb, repeating the process until you're as high as you want to be.

In bigger trees near the house I bring work equipment aloft. I'll tie off a dead limb, or a green limb that threatens the house or deck, with a separate rope running through a pulley mounted above me, then amputate limb from trunk with a bow saw and lower it gingerly eighty or a hundred feet to Marilyn, who guides it—still supported by the rope—away from the house to a safe landing. Those big limbs I eventually chainsaw for firewood, and we use some of the mossy ones to border paths and garden beds.

This work of pruning limbs at height pays me the great satisfaction of validating my life. It demonstrates, incontrovertibly, how wise I was forty years ago to drop out of college and devote myself to climbing and logging. It took several decades, but now, at last, as I hit my sixtieth birthday, I have blended the two and found my one true calling. I don't climb only to work. Once I've got a rope in a tall tree, I'll sometimes climb into its crown, unclip from the rope, and climb higher from limb to limb as I used to do as a kid, much closer to ground. Now and then I clip myself to a branch or the narrowing trunk as a safety precaution, but once well up in the treetop you would have to try hard to fall out of its brushy clutches.

Soon, maybe, I'll buy one of the hammocks designed for hanging out in trees. I would like to relax from climbing and working and simply be there, on high, losing my thoughts to the murmurous breeze and the tree's slight sway. Maybe Marilyn could be persuaded to send up cold beer and sandwiches in a bucket on a line; in return, I could lower small poems. There are mysteries up there. I might see at last the birds whose fluent songs in springtime I have heard on the ground but whose feathers I have never glimpsed, because those high revelers never come down to mix with the grosbeaks and finches. There are voles and other small creatures up in the crowns whose generations have never touched ground—the tree is their ground. If I spent a night, I might finally determine if flying squirrels, which are nocturnal, inhabit these trees—the books suggest they might well. If I were still enough, maybe a barn owl or great horned owl would glide on silent wings to perch on a nearby limb. Maybe I would dream transcendent dreams.

It's a tough thrash up the last few feet of the tallest trees, squeezing through thickets of small limbs, getting scratches on my arms and bark bits in my eyes, my hands blackened with redolent pitch. I can't climb to the very top, because at the top there is no tree — only a limber sapling dripping with pitch, sometimes studded with clenched green cones. Eleven feet in circumference near ground level, the tree rises half the length of a football field to top out in a singular needled spire, of the kind you cap with an angel at Christmas time. The tree does not leave its youth behind. The tree preserves and exalts it, lifts it skyward as the center of its great candelabra crown. To spend a moment just short of the top — the loftiest landing my body can reach, the highest limit of my home ground — looking down on roof and garden and stream bottom, on neighboring fields and scalped and wooded ridges beyond, is to sense again my own young self, to find him smiling within the aches and stiffness and rutted habits of my sixty years.

I'm not much of a flag waver, but a flag does fly from the peak of the roof on the south end of our house, over the back deck from which we look out on mossy Douglas firs and a few white oaks. It's a handsome flag, I have to say, and it makes a happy sound. When I'm digging or pruning or loafing on the deck and hear its sudden flappedy-snap in the wind, I look up and smile, as if surprised by a friend. Depending on the way the wind's blowing, I might see the flag's front side, which shows, in gold on a navy blue field, a pretty ordinary state seal with a few generic symbols — a plow, a sheaf of wheat, a pickaxe, and a sunset behind a covered wagon, thus acknowledging those who traversed the Oregon Trail and the work of the land that some of them have pursued since. The most interesting images, beneath the inevitable eagle that forms the crest of the seal, are of two sailing ships, a British man-of-war and an American trading vessel. The man-of-war is headed to the left, away from our coast, and the American ship to the right, sailing toward us. In this way we rejoice, within the crude limits of two dimensions, that the British were sent packing from this hotly contested Far Corner when American settlers established the Oregon Territory in 1848 and in 1859 entered the Union as the thirty-third state.

Of the fifty state flags, only ours, it turns out, has different images front and back. I prefer the back side. It shows, also in gold on blue, a humble beaver, facing right and seemingly in a chipper mood, chewing on a downed log he has already notched in several places. No words, just a hump-backed beaver doing his thing. The irony runs thick. The Anglo-American contest for the Far Corner was chiefly about beaver pelts, much desired for fashionable robes and hats in Europe and the American East. Before any of those who would vote for statehood had arrived in the Oregon Territory, before a single settler had made the six-month crossing from Missouri, the indigenous population of Oregon beaver had been reduced by probably ninety percent, trapped out by British and American traders in the first decades of the nineteenth century. While Oregon was still a wilderness, the animal that would be totemized on the state flag was already an endangered species. Settlement did not improve its lot—by the early twentieth century, when the state flag was adopted, the beaver had been practically exterminated—and now, a full century later, its population stands at a small fraction of its pre–Euro-American numbers. The state of beaver in the Beaver State is not prosperous.

Early American plantation owners and yeoman farmers wrote admiringly of this rodent's assiduous habits—it repairs and strengthens its constructions nightly—but were less charmed when those habits crossed purposes with their own. The human and beaver species have different ideas about which trees to take down and which tracts of land to flood, creating a nuisance now and then for present-day ranchers and farmers. Overall, though, we humans clearly have had the better of the disagreement, which would have been a fairer contest back in the Pleistocene, when an ancestral beaver the size and weight of a modern black bear, its cutting teeth six inches long—the largest rodent ever to roam the continent—lived and worked in North America.

But the modern beaver, which weighs usually no more than a fairly large dog, is plenty scrappy and tenacious; what's more, in pursuing its self-interest it does good works for the land that sustains it. Beaver numbers are on the rise these days in some heavily logged Northwestern places because they like the willows and alders—the inner bark is their favorite food—that pioneer plant succession in stripped riparian areas. The dams they build slow the erosive energy of streams, retaining moisture and nutrients in hungry and thirsty places. Before the beaver was trapped out of eastern Oregon, streams there tended to be strings of beaver-dammed pools and surrounding wetlands, the wetlands absorbing flood waters in season, keeping the water table flush, springs a-flowing, food webs thriving. A dry country was not as dry then.

And so I'm happy that the beaver honors our flag, and I think we would do well to honor it. The beaver perseveres in the face of persecution. The beaver works hard (though surely it doesn't consider its activities "work"). The beaver does what it does, and in making a home it promotes the general well-being of the country around it. Liberal with its energy, conservative with the water of life, the beaver earns its place in the intricate and populous commonwealth that we call the land. Does it love the land? Surely it loves its mate (beaver pair for life) and loves its kits, and who can say that it does not love its mud-daubed home of sticks, and its home forest—so tasty and useful!—and its home lake or stream? The beaver contributes more to watershed health than most humans do. It does not raise flags on its dams and lodges, but in my book, the beaver does indeed love the land.

Patriotism in America has been trivialized, abstracted, and forced into partisan servitude marked by shallow observances. For me, it begins where I am. Love of country, if it's to mean anything more, must first mean *country*, land, the physical ground and growth and weather and inhabitants—beaver as well as human—of the places we call home. If I can't love my home acre at Winter Creek and its partially stripped surrounding hills, and if I can't love my outlier homes in eastern Oregon and the Rogue River country at Dutch Henry Homestead, how can I possibly love my state or nation? If I can't take responsibility—imperfect as it is—for a few actual American places, how can I be a responsible American?

My love of country does extend beyond my home places, but I keep it pretty close to the ground. I love the landscape itself of Oregon and the Pacific Northwest; I love, in fact, the entire breadth of the forty-nine American states I have seen, in all their regional inflections. I love American literature and the spoken American tongue in its array of accents and dialects, its distinctive tunes and idioms, and at my best I love all who speak the language, including those I disagree with. And there are, of course, American ideas and institutions that I love and feel grateful for—the casting of ballots in free elections, the deliberations of earnest men and women in the jury room, the near-miracle of a revolutionary experiment in self-government evolving for more than two hundred years under the guidance of a Constitution stable enough to contain but dynamic enough not to overly constrain the freedoms of its people.

Why then not fly the Stars and Stripes? Because, though I believe in our democratic form of government—it is, as Winston Churchill quipped, the worst system in the world except for all the others—too often I cannot support the particular administration running the government, especially when that administration leads the country into needless war and continues warring for years without the majority consent of the American people. The Iraq War is more than five years old as I write, at the cost of about forty-two hundred American dead and thirty thousand wounded. The Vietnam War went longer, killing fifty-eight thousand Americans. Neither war was necessary to our national defense. Four thousand or fifty-eight, squandering the lives of our young men and women, and the lives of foreign innocents across the oceans, cannot possibly earn security. It can earn only a future of more such wars. We would do better to spend our labor and treasure strengthening national security at home, including the security of the land itself—healthy watersheds, flourishing forests, clean energy sources, and a generally defter, more imaginative, more responsible membership in our home places.

My patriotism, I know, will not satisfy some members of my community and some Americans of other communities. I can only say in return that I cannot honor a patriotism that idealizes a heroic American identity and considers failure to worship *that* America, right or wrong, as tantamount to sin. I suggest that dissent from acts and policies that I consider wrong affirms my best hopes for what our society can be, that it expresses love of country more meaningfully than wearing a flag pin or holding hand over heart during the national anthem. I concede not a drop of patriotic superiority to those who make a cult of such customs even as they condemn dissent. But I also say this: Despite our differences, all earnest men and women can and should hold in common a love for the American land itself, the land that bears our footsteps, yields our sustenance, and holds the remains of our dead, the land that spreads scarred but beautiful before us in its ample variety, the land that will thrive if only we realize that we are part of it.

I don't like everything about the state of Oregon, either. Let me count the ways. We're too hard on beaver, salmon, old-growth trees, and other members of the commonwealth with far more seniority than we have. Our state capitol in Salem looks like a bowling trophy or a misbegotten birthday cake. In many localities we are selfishly starving our schools of funding and thereby stunting our future. We are addicted to amending our state constitution with one piddling provision after another. Our history includes shameful episodes, not completely acknowledged, of killing and uprooting Native Americans and of racist acts and policies toward African Americans. Ours is one of two states in the Union that ban self-service gasoline, preferring that eighteen-year-olds making minimum wage inhale the benzene and other toxic vapors while we relax in the driver's seat comfortably insulated from the stink of carbon consumption.

And lastly, for a largely moderate populace in a moderate climate in an out-of-the-way far corner of the country, we are a culturally and politically divided people—a mostly conservative rural population that practices or did practice the traditional economies of working the land, and a mostly liberal and environmentalist urban and suburban population that supports itself by newer economies, while relying, of course, on products of the old. The two Oregons are still learning to talk to each other, which is only to say that like Americans of any state or locality, we have work to do.

Marilyn and I have seen one beaver in this area. He was scuttling around in shallow water by a culvert just up West Sheffler Road, where a small stream comes down from clearcut slopes and pecker-pole plantations on the ridge above. A hundred years ago, Douglas firs five and six feet in diameter stood up there, and still larger trees down here. Now the stream runs through willow thickets, cloudy with suspended clay. As we watched that beaver, he seemed more irritated than enthused. He paused now and then, as if thinking, "What the hell am I supposed to do with *this*?" We didn't see him again, but peering upstream into the brushy woods a month or two later I thought I glimpsed a pool that hadn't been there before. It's posted private property, so I can't go in to confirm, but I think our irritable toothy neighbor decided to stay and go to work. I like that. He takes an interest in this scraped and battered countryside, and so do I. He does some good for our common watershed and I try to as well. If he causes a little trouble from time to time, well, I do too. Neither of us may be an exemplary citizen, but the way I see it, the beaver is a patriot and so am I.

Thirty years ago, with a nine-year-old friend, I climbed a tall ponderosa pine on a ranch in eastern Oregon. Starting from the roof of a shed and roped together, Nathan below, we found plenty of limbs for our hands and feet. Nathan's black hair was full of bark flakes and he was chewing a gob of pine pitch as I belayed him up to a kind of natural crow's nest atop the tree. There his exuberance turned quiet, solemn, as he looked north across the road at his family's red frame house, elms and cottonwoods around it, his dog asleep in the driveway. He saw familiar alfalfa fields and fields of oats, and in a far pasture his father's brown pickup creeping with a load of hay, the Herefords and Angus following. Up the mild grade to the west, he saw the pond where he and his four brothers fished and swam and played hockey, Bryant Mountain blue in the distance beyond. And close alongside to the east ranged Goodlow Rim, its junipered slopes and crumbling basalt all flushed with sun, angling away northwest toward far-away Yainax Butte, and stepping down to the south to the incised mouth of Miller Creek Canyon, which held the remains of a Prohibition still and fossils from an ancient sea. As we felt in our bellies the easy sway of the ponderosa, Nathan looked at the places and things he knew from the ground and saw them composed, made whole in his vision. "Let's stay," he said. "Let's stay a long time."

I was in love with mountains then, alpine lakes, wooded wilderness places where I camped and climbed, but I never recognized a particular landscape as home until I came to live on that ranch in Langell Valley (the *g* is soft), east of Klamath Falls. What is it about a piece of country that takes us in and feels its way into the heart? I liked well enough the gently hilled terrain of Maryland where I had grown up, and the Blue Ridge of northern Virginia where my parents owned a weekend cabin, and the Alleghenies further to the west, but nothing held me or called me back to those places after I'd said goodbye. My father's country, south-west Missouri on the fringe of the Ozarks, I felt intensely as *his* place, my aunts' place, the place of the grandparents and great-grandparents I never knew, not as my own. Same with the coast of Maine, where I spent parts of many summers at my maternal grandfather's vacation house, and where my mother returned to live late in her life — great country, her country, not mine. As a college student and dropout I got to know western Oregon a little and found it verdant and lovely, especially the rocky coast — so different from the crowded, hot sand beaches of Delaware and Florida — but I was exactly what the Wilderness Act of 1964 had intended, "a visitor who does not remain." The land was a recreational playground, not a home.

It makes a difference, of course, who you are when you arrive, what you bring to a new landscape. I was thirty when I came to the ranch, had been knocking around through my twenties working at jobs I didn't care about, falling in love a couple of times, moving on. Maybe I was ready to settle down. By then I was coaxing myself to sit at a table and write, and sometimes to sit again the next day and try to see what was good in what I had written and what wasn't, and how I might make it better. And what did I write about? Coyotes, sagebrush, horned owls, the fiercely glittering midnight stars, the incandescent sundown light on Goodlow Rim. I wrote about the land itself, and I wrote with an unprecedented suspicion that though none of that land belonged to me, I might belong to it.

I was reading Theodore Roethke by then, and a couplet from one of his poems echoed through me as I tried to write what I hoped were poems:

> Myself is what I wear.
> I keep the spirit spare.

Spare were the ponderosa pines, sparser than the dense forests of conifers west of the mountains and the leafy hardwood forests I'd grown up in. Spare were the junipers, homely and stalwart, in loose array on the slow rise west of the little house I rented for fifty a month, and eastward up the rocky shortgrass slopes of Goodlow, each tree casting its own distinct shadow as the passing clouds cast theirs. There was something civilized and welcoming in the way trees and creatures and human beings as well apportioned themselves in the land. The country presented itself in particulars — *this* juniper, *this* lichened rock, this golden eagle riding the thermals, this series of ecstatic, wailing coyote cries in the deep of the night — and this way that solitary things and happenings invited my attention seemed to show me traces at least of my own singularity, a sense of what I was and could be or could at least hope to be.

The drama of the western Oregon landscape is of coast and mountains and the profuse exuberance of its biota, the many shades and textures and stories of green. This abundance climaxes in the surviving remnants of old-growth rainforest, whose behemoth, mossy-trunked cedars and hem-locks and Sitka spruces tower in stillness, many of them tilted toward their eventual fall; and after the fall, as they decay, they host seedlings and saplings that will one day tower in the same stillness, the same clear sun-light filtered by needled boughs and the understory of alders and big-leaf maples. Death rises in these forests in a slow green riot, measured in cen-turies, abetted by plentiful rain and snowmelt that the forest conserves in its sponge of rotting wood and litter-fall and fragrant black soil. Westside old growth, which my home grove increasingly resembles, and the climate that makes old growth — those long, gray, rainy, and misty months — turn me inward, toward thought, reverie, memory. It's reading weather, writing weather, weather for a fire in the hearth and a pot roast on the stove.

Eastern Oregon, at higher elevations where moisture is sufficient, has old growth forest of a different character: grassy parklands of tall, tilted ponderosa pines, their orange bark scored with deep black furrows, their crowns often singing with wind in a higher, more whistling voice than I hear in Douglas firs. Huddles of aspens flag spring and seep, their leaves trembling in breezes that human skin can scarcely perceive. In these woods I want to walk and holler. My awareness sweeps out of me like a wind of its own, this mood encouraged by a far more generous allot-ment of sunshine than we're used to on the wet side. The drama of eastern Oregon, its steppe and desert and forests too, is defined by distance — the long, lonesome views, the shifting cloud-and-lightscape of the sky, where you can watch the weather forming a long way off. Those distances open me up. As I heard a woman once say in a Chiloquin bar, "Over here, I've got room to *fluff.*"

Moist, enclosing, rainforest stillness. Breezy spaciousness of vibrant pines. Maybe one forest stirs my soul, which I conceive of as a creature of depth and stillness, and the other stirs my spirit, which to me is the lively breath of being. I love both forests, I love both sides of my distinctly divided state, but I confess I love the dry side more. The country that Nathan and I looked out on from the tall pine, and the country for many miles around it, is the landscape of my heart—and happily, my heart has a home there. Nathan and three of his four brothers have left the ranch to pursue their livelihoods. So have their parents, Roger and Karen, who now live in Eugene, not far from Marilyn and me. We have been close friends for thirty years. They still own the ranch, along with the son who lives there. Three generations of their family—they, their sons with wives and children—still return to spend time there, and so do we. Marilyn and I have an interest in a cottage that sits on the site of the crumbling house, long since burnt to the ground, where I lived and first tried to write poems in the 1970s. The ponderosa I climbed with Nathan stands a hundred feet away. We are bound to the places we love by the nature of the land, and we are bound by the people we come to know and love as part of the land.

My friend Frank Boyden, a ceramist, printmaker, and Oregon native who lives on the coast at Cascade Head, decades ago used to stop his car at the border and do a little roadside dance when returning home, he was so glad to live in this state. Frank's knees were better then. My knees, as I hit sixty, are pretty spry, the one of bone and cartilage and the one of titanium and plastic, but I'm too self-conscious to dance in the view of passing motorists. I'm not a native, either, but I feel as Frank does when I see the WELCOME TO OREGON sign. . . .

After ten weeks away, teaching in Virginia then gradually traveling west again, the truck and I come to the Snake River crossing at last. We ditch Interstate 84 at Ontario and we're back in Oregon, cruising west on U.S. 20. The flat fields, sour with the scent of last year's onions, are just furzing up with new green this first week of March. At Vale, where there is no vale (and no Ontario in Ontario, founded by a homesick Canadian), we pick up the Malheur River with its raw cutbanks, a few mergansers drifting the easy current. Low blue hills ahead turn warmly brown as they gather us in, still half asleep in their winter drab, and the road weaves up into country spotted with junipers and crops of lava. It looked the same, I bet, but for the cheat grass, to the pioneers, and to Indians long before

THE WAGES OF MORTALITY

them. A magpie, sharp-tailored in black and white, flies from a juniper fencepost; Herefords hulk impassive behind barbed wire. We ease down to Juntura, where two forks of the Malheur join, Bible Church at one end of town, little brick Catholic at the other.

The highway climbs again, past a white ranch house with its poplar windbreak, hay baled up in gigantic rolls in the fields. Over Drinkwater Pass, I stop at the mainstem Malheur crossing to pay my respects to two beaver I met a couple years back. I spent an hour watching them at dusk as they spread their vees in the easy water, slapping a tail on the river now and then to let me know how much they appreciated my visit. Today they're not in evidence—like me, beaver tend to be nocturnal—and no sign of lodgings. If they haven't been trapped or shot, maybe they've settled somewhere else on this hard-used ranching river.

A few miles on, it's Stinkingwater Pass. Drink, Stink—the names might have saved your life, back when—then down mildly in curves to the northern fringe of the Great Basin, speeding over shallow streams flowing south to the marshes of Malheur Lake, where raucous geese may have started to gather, where environmentalist cohorts and I were picketed once by folks from the region who took exception to our desire for new wilderness areas hereabouts. The pavement shoots dead ahead on the dry floor of a vast Pleistocene lake, the truck running fast and free. A windmill, three pintos nosing the sparse grass. Fifty miles south, Steens Mountain stands in snowy solitude, called Snow Mountain on old maps, its sheer eastern face rising five thousand feet above the Alvord Desert. Then Burns, which now boasts not one, not two, but three espresso shops, plus a McDonald's and a mall called Steens Mountain Plaza. Too bad not even Burns is immune, but the coffee, pretty good coffee, rides warm in my belly.

The truck and I drive on, south then west out of town, and the broad country takes on a roll. Too early in spring for sage grouse strutting near Sagehen Summit, and way too early for camas flowers to blue-up in the swales near Riley, where you might see sandhill cranes. U. S. 20 tends northwest in broad winding curves, rising and falling past Squaw, Glass, and Hampton Buttes, all still traced with snow. Phone poles pace alongside, some of them skewed; the mottled cheat grass flats and lazy slopes turn rich with evening sun. Three crows, a tan doublewide. And now on the western horizon three small points, like arrowhead tips—the Sisters? They dip away and pop up again with the roll of the land, then rise in full—the snowy blue Sisters all right, backlit with a saffron sky, Broken Top to their south. We pass the eye-blink town of Brothers, named by sheepherders watching the regal Sisters from three small bumps in the desert, then on through dusk and darkness into Bend.

After scrambled eggs in the morning we vacate Oregon's new Recreationville. It's always been a crossroads—settlers forded the Deschutes River here, at a double curve called Farewell Bend—but the traffic's a mite thicker now. The highway leads on, just north of northwest, past nouveau mansions and fresh manufactured homes on sagebrush flats, with a mountain view hard to match anywhere. The Sisters rise near and huge off the truck's port bow—the two who like to talk to each other, the third who keeps to herself. Next to the north is Mount Washington, which I've climbed four times, from this angle a rock pinhead on square shoulders. Then Three-Fingered Jack, two fingers missing; ten-thousand-foot Mount Jefferson, fat with snow; and Hood hunkered in haze to the distant north. Landmarks to Natives and trappers and pioneers, landmarks today. Some western states are strewn with peaks. Ours are few and singular.

Junipers give way to ponderosa pines as the truck hums up the grade, the first tall trees since . . . well, since leaving Oregon, ten weeks ago. Then mountain hemlocks, lodgepole pines, and Santiam Pass, and we're headed south on 126, the truck running strong, like a horse that just sniffed home. Down and down the continuous canyon of wet-barked Douglas firs, each in its own snow well, dirty snow mounded along the shoulder. The McKenzie River, first maker of this trail, gives off white flashes through the woods. From Blue River on, the upper slopes show off their bad buzzcuts. (Myself, I like my mountains shaggy.) We hit the flats at Leaburg, where precocious blooms speckle a few fruit trees and sheep and llamas graze the pastures. The grass is shockingly green, and soon comes the weather that makes it so. Clear sailing three-and-a-half days from Chicago, two thousand miles of late-winter sun, and now, my dear, gray Willamette Valley, sprinkling rain.

Skirting north of Eugene we roll on, past cormorants airing their wings and a great blue heron in the lake by the Long Tom River, our home watershed. Pastures, woodlots, a hazelnut farm, the road steering me and the truck along known curves and grades. One new clearcut on Butler Road—the usual mess, but this one has opened a lovely southwest view of the bumpy Coast Range, now drifted with strands of mist. A straightaway, two little hills, a last left turn, and we're crunching the home gravel. I pat the truck on its dashboard, switch off the motor, and clamber out stiff and happy. The Douglas firs are right where I left them. The tallest were putting down roots at about the time my father's grandfather shipped out from Prussia in the 1860s for a new life in Missouri. The smallest are probably sixty or so, youngsters like me. They'll be standing here in their own quiet, I hope, gathering moss and stature, long after Marilyn and I are gone.

But right now she has heard the truck arrive and is very much here, all five feet ten inches of her, as lovely as ever with her red hair and smiling face. We share a long hug beneath the trees and then take a stroll around the acre. Winter Creek is in season, flowing with its small but songful voice. The few birds we see—chickadees, nuthatches, siskins—are year-round residents, like us; the bright swarms of goldfinches and grosbeaks are still more than a month away. Twigs and boughs from the Douglas firs, scraps of lungwort and wisps of old man's beard, and blackened leaves from the oaks and fruit trees litter the sleeping grass. The earth has gathered the life of the place to itself, hinting its plans in the sweet odor of duff and soil that we breathe in with the moist air—news of stirrings in the roots, of trillium and fiddleheads preparing to rise, good news of this ground from which flowers and forest and even words sometimes, like these, will find their way.

Coda

POWER HITTER

In the Maryland suburb of Washington, D.C., where I was a boy in the 1950s, we played baseball on a rough field in a bottomland commons. The area around home plate — I think we had a real, store-bought plate, though I could be wrong — was a mire of sand worn loose by the sneakered feet of countless batters. Three immovably embedded stones served as bases, second a good ten feet farther from first than it was from third. There were other rocks, and hummocks and holes, throughout the field. Anything hit on the ground with a bit of authority had an excellent chance of bad-hopping through the infield for a base hit.

In the outfield there were no fences. A ball hit deep to left-center usually came down in poison ivy or honeysuckle thickets along the creek, and the outfielder might still be pawing through the brush — no ground-rule doubles in our game — as the batter burned around third for home.

My brother Jim and one or two of his friends could reach those thickets on occasion. Jim, who batted left-handed, once cracked an enormous drive that cleared a few small trees on a steep slope in far right field and left the bottomland altogether. The teams argued whether it had come down fair or foul. Who could tell? It took a twenty-minute search to find the ball — our only one — where it had come to rest in someone's backyard flowers.

At ten years old I didn't have that strength or eye. My swings, also left-handed, usually produced ground balls or soft line drives, a few of which went for singles. In one game I hit a grounder down the first base line that somehow got past the first baseman and bounced off the stick we had shoved in a hole for a foul pole.

"That's a home run!" I yelled. "It hits the foul pole, it's a homer!"

My brother's friends groaned and hooted. "That's if you hit it on the fly, dork," said one of them. "In a real ball park."

"This is a ball park," I muttered, drawing a disgusted silence.

I longed for the day when I could bury a ball in the sky, when I could hit the hard line drives or deep flies my brother could—or even, I dreamed, the colossal home run I had seen Ted Williams launch at Griffith Stadium, the white ball shooting off the sliver of his bat with the thrust of a sharp line drive but impossibly high and deep, still climbing, it seemed, as it cleared the lofty green centerfield wall and left the stadium altogether, to carom among cars and building fronts in the dirty streets of Northeast Washington. I imagined it then and still do today, bat meeting pitch so cleanly your hands feel nothing, not a stitch of vibration, and wherever the ball comes down it has left the confines of your life.

Time is a boy's best hope, but it's hard to believe in. You have no power. Time alone can get you some, but time scarcely moves, withholding its favors in a vague and distant future. In the meantime you have no place of your own, only your room, and even that isn't yours—it's on loan from parents who can open the door whenever they want and tell you what to do or not to do. School, whatever its rewards for a goody-good student such as you, is a concentration camp you can only escape when they let you. You're tall for your age but really you're small, smaller than your brother, smaller than anyone who matters. There's nothing of importance to the world that you can do.

So, you assert yourself in ways the world doesn't know. You make a bow from a notched green stick and a piece of string, arrows from whatever nearly straight twigs you can find, and you go down to stalk frogs in the creek. You spin your steel-pointed top with fiercer and fiercer pulls of its cord, trying to drill holes in your bedroom floor. You take a pencil and bore out the core of a small green apple and insert your last firecracker, then steal matches from your father's dresser, put on your helmet and head out to play war, smirking as you think of the others with their fake grenades. You grab a foam pillow from the rec-room sofa and slug it and slam it to the floor as you watch wrestling on the black-and-white TV, Gorgeous George and Haystacks Calhoun. You lay pennies on the tracks by Macarthur Boulevard and wait for the trolley to clatter swayingly by, throwing sparks from its overhead wire, then rush down to see if you've accomplished at last a perfect mash job, Abe Lincoln a faint, even, vast-headed coppery ghost.

Once in a while you get a chance in an unlikely place. You smile, entering the upstairs bathroom, if one of your father's Chesterfield butts is floating in the toilet. You assess your firepower, and if it's not ample you go to the kitchen for Kool-Aid and wait, hoping no one needs to go in the meantime. When you know you are ready you assume your stance over the theater of battle and take aim, holding it back between finger and thumb, and then you let loose a hard volley. The butt might blow up right away if your aim is precise and it's been soaking a while, but more often you have to track it with careful, relentless fire as it scoots around its suddenly turbulent pond. To waver even once from the target is to risk failure as your ammunition dwindles. You must flay the sopped paper, spill every brown shred of unburnt tobacco, and even, to do the job right, break up the black tip that's been hardened by burning.

You pursue this mission with such purpose and passion not to protest your father's habit of smoking. You like your father, and it's the 1950s — he and your mother and most of their friends all smoke and drink. You don't hate them for it, you envy them. You may fret from time to time that you will never attain the height and weight to admit you to the world of men, but if that spurs you on in the present operation it never bobs to the surface of your ten-year-old mind. The truth is, you track and destroy the cigarette butt for the same reason that George Leigh-Mallory climbed Everest — because it is there, because you have the equipment to do it, and because, your sortie accomplished, the day shines a bit brighter as you run down the stairs, jumping the last five to the landing.

Notes and Thanks

With love and gratitude I thank Marilyn, who makes this literary cottage industry possible.

Great thanks also to Jack Shoemaker, my editor; to Adam Krefman and the entire staffs of Counterpoint and Publishers Group West; and to John Laursen of Press-22 in Portland, book designer extraordinaire and a sharp-eyed editor in his own right.

The following persons, books, and periodicals were of help in the creation and previous publication of the essays in *The Far Corner*. The imperfections of the essays remain entirely my own.

To the Reader

Stewart Holbrook, *Far Corner: A Personal View of the Pacific Northwest* (New York: Macmillan, 1952).

Brian Booth, editor, *Wildmen, Wobblies & Whistle Punks: Stewart Holbrook's Lowbrow Northwest* (Corvallis: Oregon State University Press, 1992).

Cuttings

An earlier version was first published in *Beloved of the Sky*, edited by John Ellison (Seattle: Broken Moon Press, 1992), and won the Andres Berger Award for Creative Nonfiction in 1994. The essay was reprinted in *American Nature Writing 1995*, edited by John A. Murray (San Francisco: Sierra Club Books, 1995), and in other anthologies. Most recently "Cuttings" appeared in *Working the Woods, Working the Sea*, edited by Finn Wilcox and Jerry Gorsline (Empty Bowl Press, 2008).

I wish this essay were no longer relevant. Since its first publication the timber cut on federal lands in the Northwest has been substantially reduced, but the old-growth reserves and roadless area protections won in the 1990s are under continual pressure from both within and without the federal land-management agencies. Steep-slope clearcutting has continued apace on private holdings, much of the timber going for export. We in the Northwest are still a long way from achieving sustainable forestry.

Wavewash

I thank Ona Siporin, Jim Hepworth, and John Moat for reading and commenting on this essay. Thanks also to *Mountain Gazette* for rejecting it, in much cruder form, in 1979, and for encouraging me to make it better.

Robinson Jeffers, "The Eye." In *Robinson Jeffers: Selected Poems* (New York: Vintage Books, 1965).

A Word in Favor of Rootlessness

First published, in slightly different form, in *Orion* 14, no. 4 (Autumn 1995), edited by Chip Blake. Reprinted in *Nature Writing: The Tradition in English*, edited by Robert Finch and John Elder (New York: W. W. Norton, 2002), and in other anthologies. Most recently the essay appeared in *Writing the Journey: Essays, Stories, and Poems on Travel*, edited by David Espey (New York: Pearson Longman, 2005).

Thanks to John Haines for his thoughts on this essay and to Aina Niemela, then of *Orion*, for an excellent suggestion regarding its ending. Jack Hicks, director of the Art of the Wild Writers Conference in Squaw Valley, gave me the opportunity to give the talk that became the essay.

Coyote Was Going There: Indian Literature of the Oregon Country, edited by Jarold Ramsey (Seattle: University of Washington Press, 1980).

In Praise of Darkness

First published in *Southwest Review* 92, no. 4 (Fall 2007). My thanks to editor-in-chief Willard Spiegelman. A different version appeared as "Night Writing" in *Resurgence* (England), edited by Satish Kumar.

Paul Bogard, who included this essay in his welcome anthology *Let There Be Night: Testimony on Behalf of the Dark* (Reno: University of Nevada Press, 2008), had several helpful suggestions. I am also grateful to Jay Fliegelman (1949–2007), professor of English at Stanford University, a brilliant Americanist and electrifying lecturer.

A. Roger Ekirch, *At Day's Close: Night in Times Past* (New York: W.W. Norton, 2005).

Henry Thoreau, June 11 and August 5, 1851. In *H. D. Thoreau: A Writer's Journal*, edited by Laurence Stapleton (New York: Dover Publications, 1960).

St. John of the Cross, "The Dark Night." In *The Soul Is Here for its Own Joy*, edited by Robert Bly (Hopewell, NJ: The Ecco Press, 1995).

Henry Vaughan, "The Night." In *The Norton Anthology of Poetry* (New York: W.W. Norton, 1983).

Robinson Jeffers, "Night." In *Robinson Jeffers: Selected Poems*.

Emily Dickinson, "As imperceptibly as Grief." In *Final Harvest: Emily Dickinson's Poems*, edited by Thomas H. Johnson (Boston: Little, Brown, 1961).

X. J. Kennedy, "Ars Poetica." In *Peeping Tom's Cabin: Comic Verse 1928–2008* (Rochester, NY: BOA Editions, 2007).

Oregon Rivers: A Suite in Six Parts

The essays in this section are slightly revised from their original publication in *Oregon Rivers*, where they accompanied photographs by Larry

N. Olson (Englewood, CO: Westcliffe Publishers, 1997). Larry's image of the Wallowa River, in the Fishtrap country of northeastern Oregon, graces the cover of this book. An earlier version of "Beginnings" appeared in *Portland* magazine, edited by Brian Doyle.

To my many acknowledgments in *Oregon Rivers* I add additional thanks to fluvial geomorphologist Gordon Grant, of the Pacific Northwest Research Station, U. S. Forest Service, in Corvallis, and to geologist and old friend Jim Jackson, for his close readings of Chapter West in the book of North America. Beyond the present work, both helped immensely with my contributions to *Home Ground: Language for an American Landscape*, edited by Barry Lopez and Debra Gwartney (San Antonio: Trinity University Press, 2006), in which there wasn't room to acknowledge them.

The Prankster-in-Chief Moves On

First published in different form as "The Prankster Moves On: Remembering Ken Kesey" in *Open Spaces* 4, no. 3 (Winter 2001–2002), edited by Penny Harrison, and later in *Spit in the Ocean: All About Kesey*, edited by Ed McClanahan (New York: Penguin, 2003). Jeff Barnard, Wendell Berry, Marilyn Daniel, and Ed McClanahan offered helpful comments.

Jackson Benson, *Wallace Stegner: His Life and Work* (New York: Viking, 1996).

Ken Kesey, "The Day After Superman Died." In *Demon Box* (New York: Penguin Group, 1987).

Wallace Stegner and Richard W. Etulain, *Conversations with Wallace Stegner on Western History and Literature* (Salt Lake City: University of Utah Press, 1983).

Wallace Stegner's Hunger for Wholeness

First published in *High Plains Literary Review* (Fall 1997) and shortly afterward in *Wallace Stegner and the Continental Vision*, edited by Curt Meine (Washington, D.C.: Island Press, 1997). Thanks to Jim Hepworth,

Curt Meine, and Jack Shoemaker for suggestions along the way.

Wallace Stegner, "The Sound of Mountain Water." In *The Sound of Mountain Water: The Changing American West* (New York: Dutton, 1980).

Wallace Stegner, *Wolf Willow: A History, a Story, and a Memory of the Last Plains Frontier* (New York: Viking, 1962).

Kay Bonnetti, *Interview with Wallace Stegner*, Audio Prose Library, February 1987.

Wallace Stegner, "On the Writing of History." In *The Sound of Mountain Water*.

Wallace Stegner, "Letter, Much Too Late." In *Where the Bluebird Sings to the Lemonade Springs: Living and Writing in the West* (New York: Random House, 1992).

Wallace Stegner, "Ansel Adams and the Search for Perfection." In *One Way to Spell Man: Essays with a Western Bias* (New York: Doubleday, 1982).

Wallace Stegner, "Finding the Place: A Migrant Childhood." In *Where the Bluebird Sings to the Lemonade Springs*.

Wallace Stegner, "A Desert Shelf." In *One Way to Spell Man*.

Wallace Stegner and Richard Etulain, *Conversations with Wallace Stegner on Western History and Literature*.

"Creative Nonfiction" and the Province of Personal Narrative

First published in a different form in *Weber Studies* 16, no. 2 (Winter 1999), guest edited by Louis Owens. My thanks to Louis, now in memory, for inviting this essay and helping me improve it. I wrote much of it while a fellow at Oregon State University's Center for the Humanities in 1997–1998. I am grateful to Wendy Madar and to the late Peter Copek, founder of the center.

John Burroughs, *Riverby* (Boston: Houghton Mifflin, 1894).

Gerald M. Edelman, *Bright Air, Brilliant Fire: On the Matter of the Mind* (New York: Basic Books, 1992).

George Orwell, "A Hanging." In *The Penguin Essays of George Orwell*, edited by Bernard Crick (New York: Penguin Classics, 1994).

The River

First published in a different form as "The Flow of Life" in *Audubon* 104, no. 1 (January/February 2002). Mary-Powel Thomas, then with *Audubon*, was a friendly and helpful editor.

Solitude in a Dry Season

Developed from "Dutch Henry Journal," published in *Writing Nature* (Summer 1995). Great thanks to friend and editor J. Parker Huber, and to the Boyden clan for their generous loan of Dutch Henry Homestead.

Emily Dickinson, "Further in Summer than the Birds." In *Final Harvest: Emily Dickinson's Poems*.

Sir Philip Sidney, Sonnet 1, "Astrophel and Stella." In *The Norton Anthology of Poetry*.

Henry Thoreau, December 12, 1851. In *H. D. Thoreau: A Writer's Journal*.

The Mother of Beauty

My heartfelt gratitude to Renee Stacey, Gabe Hamilton, Roger Hamilton, Molly Juillerat, John Stacey, Marilyn Daniel, and especially to Susie Juillerat, who taught us in both her living and her dying. Thanks to Satish Kumar for his mother's story and to friend and doctor Dan Patel for useful comments. This essay evolved from a talk I gave in 1999 as the Allen M. Boyden Memorial Lecturer at St. Vincent Hospital in Portland.

Wendell Berry, "The Old Elm Tree by the River." In *Collected Poems* (San Francisco: North Point Press, 1985).

"Coyote and Eagle Go to the Land of the Dead." In *Coyote Was Going There.*

A Word in Favor of Rootedness

Elements of this essay derive from "Homing in on Oregon," published in the *Eugene Weekly* (December 14, 1995), then edited by Debra Gwartney; from "Turnings of Seasons," published in *Sierra* and in *The Earth at Our Doorstep: Contemporary Writers Celebrate the Landscapes of Home*, edited by Annie Stine (San Francisco: Sierra Club Books, 1996); and from my afterword to *Oregon Then & Now*, by Steve Terrill and Thomas Robinson (Englewoood, CO: Westcliffe Publishers, 2000).

An excerpt from the essay as published here appeared in *Oregon Humanities*, edited by Kathleen Holt. Thanks to Marilyn Daniel for her suggestions and to Roger Hamilton for the Pleistocene beaver.

Bernard DeVoto, editor, *The Journals of Lewis and Clark* (Boston: Mariner Books, 1997).

William G. Loy and Stuart Allan, *Atlas of Oregon* (Eugene: University of Oregon Press, 2001).

Theodore Roethke, "Open House." In *The Collected Poems of Theodore Roethke* (New York: Random House, 1974).

Lewis A. McArthur, *Oregon Geographic Names*, sixth edition (Portland: Oregon Historical Society Press, 1992).

Power Hitter

First published in *Open Spaces* 5, no. 2.